Exploring the Magic of Your Hero's Journey

By

Pat Edwards

The author and publisher gratefully acknowledge the following artists and writers for their permission to reprint their work in this publication. Thanks also to the individuals profiled throughout this book for allowing us to share in their Hero's Journey.

"Amondo and the Baobab" by Hélène Ducharme and Hamadoun Kassogué excerpted with permission from the authors.

Excerpt(s) from THE ONCE AND FUTURE KING by T. H. White, copyright 1938, 1939,
1940, © 1958 by T. H. White. Used by permission of G. P. Putnam's Sons, an imprint of Penguin
Publishing Group, a division of Penguin Random House LLC. All rights reserved.

Excerpt(s) from THE HEROINE'S JOURNEY, by Maureen Murdock, © 1990. Reprinted by arrangement with Shambhala Publications, Inc., Boulder, CO. www.shambhala.com.

Excerpt(s) from WOMAN'S WORK by Dominique Christina, © 2015. Used with permission of Sounds True Publishing, 413 S. Arthur Avenue, Louisville, CO. www.soundstrue.com

Printed in the United States of America
First Printing, 2017
ISBN 978-0-9993053-1-7

FYD Publishing
609 Seventh St.
Waunakee, WI 53597

Table of Contents

We Are the Same, You and Me

An Introduction to the Magic that Is Your Hero's Journey

*"All journeys have secret destinations of which
the traveler is unaware."—Martin Buber*

I am so happy to have you with me on a Hero's Journey.

I really do believe we are the same. Our differences are teeny-tiny. You know there is something bigger for you to do, something that makes a difference. I know that for me, too.

You may think you are fragile, but you're not. You may feel broken in parts, but you're not. You may think of yourself as not quite good enough, but you are.

You can do a Hero's Journey because we're going to do it together. I'm going to guide you so you can see how you can take control of the Journey no matter where you are on it. I can be your guide, because I've walked this path for a while now.

You can go on a Hero's Journey on purpose and with a purpose great or small. I believe you can define it if you choose to. You can Journey to where you want to go.

It might take a long time to see the whole Journey as good, but you will.

Oh, and one more thing, sweetie. It will be the hardest thing you ever learn to do, but you *will* learn to trust yourself, and you *will* see how amazing you are.

What Is the Hero's Journey?

In 1949, Joseph Campbell wrote *The Hero with a Thousand Faces*. Campbell noticed that myths, stories, and legends throughout time, and from around the world, all follow a similar pattern. He named this pattern the "monomyth," or "the Hero's Journey." He saw these stories, as I do, as proof of the unity of consciousness.

Every Hero's Journey starts with an ordinary person in the Ordinary World. Every Hero's Journey has twelve stages. They're not perfectly linear. The stages rarely start and end neatly, they can overlap, and can vary greatly in duration, but every stage is there. We're going to go into more depth as we explore each stage.

Sort of a Glossary

I will use certain terms throughout the book. In some cases, I use them a little differently than the dictionary does. Understanding how I use these terms will help you understand the concepts behind them, and it will help you see your own Journey more clearly.

Campbell—Joseph Campbell, 1904-87. American mythologist, writer, and lecturer, best known for his work in comparative mythology and comparative religion, in which he describes how the stories of Heroes across cultures share an archetypal pattern. Campbell is also well known for his admonition to "Follow your bliss."

Fractal—Defined as a curve or geometric figure, each part of which has the same statistical character as the whole. Think of a fern and mentally zoom in to a single fern frond. Now zoom into the frond leaflet, called a pinna. Get your magnifying glass and look at each individual pinnule on the pinna. The pattern of the fern repeats no matter how large or small your view of the plant. That's fractal. Your Hero's Journey is also fractal. Smaller-scale journeys fit into larger, even whole-life duration journeys. Yet they all follow the same pattern.

2

Her—The feminine pronoun. I made a deliberate decision to use the feminine pronoun wherever it would be grammatically correct to use the masculine. Women aren't acculturated to see themselves as the Hero, so I want to encourage them. Men can read this book, of course, and make the pronoun change in their heads.

Journey—Shorthand for the Hero's Journey, with the full twelve stages as defined by Joseph Campbell.

Jung—Carl Jung, 1875–1961, Swiss psychiatrist and founder of analytical psychology. His work influenced Campbell's interpretation of myth and archetypes.

Monomyth—Another name for the Hero's Journey. It can be described as the common template for stories that typify the Hero's Journey.

Rest Stop—Every Journey needs places and times for resting. A **Rest Stop** is the place designated for stretching, deep breaths, rubbing your eyes, and the critical bio-break. Take a short time to withdraw, spend time alone and self-inventory. To truly rest, get as far into nature as you can and put all of your devices away for as long as you can. You can look back from where (and whence) you came. Then you can look forward to the horizon.

Stage—The dictionary defines stage as "one of a series of positions or stations, one above the other." Your Hero's Journey has twelve stages. These stages, however, are not distinct, equal in length, or equal in intensity. The stages can overlap, too. It's only when you look back that you can see the stage clearly.

Story—A myth, legend, fairy tale, book, movie . . . there are so many different ways to say the same thing. I'll use the word *story* for all of them. Using this word levels the "truthiness" for all.

Visioning Meditation—This is my term for a shamanic practice I do regularly and speak about in several places as I share my own story. To do a visioning meditation, I set aside an hour with no interruptions and sit in a comfortable chair. I listen to music (usually drumming) and cover my eyes with a sleep mask. I begin with rhythmic, circular breathing to induce a trance-like state. As I see color waves and shapes, I follow them until clearer images show themselves to me.

Chapter 1. You've Already Done a Hero's Journey, and You Can Do It Again

"There are only two or three human stories, and they go on repeating themselves as fiercely as if they had never happened before."—Willa Cather

I am on a Hero's Journey I chose deliberately, and it's about time! At the time I'm writing this, I am actually on three separate Journeys. Each is in a different stage. The first Journey is writing this book. Since you're reading the book, you know that one is near completion. The second Journey is overcoming compulsive eating. This one is extremely challenging, but I have a twelve-step program to help me. My third Journey is becoming a practicing shaman. As I write this initial chapter I have added mentors and am proceeding through the Tests and Trials stage.

I am so very grateful you are coming with me.

I started college nearly ten years after I graduated from high school. I was an adult, no longer dependent on my parents. I was excited and also frightened. How would I possibly pay for the tuition, the books, and *living* at the same time? I thought the other students would be younger, smarter, and more aware than I was. Their last mathematics class would have been three months ago. Mine was ten years ago. While sitting in the administration offices, I heard someone mention a "blue book." What was a blue book? Did I need one right now? All of the other students would know every answer when called upon. I just knew I'd look pathetically dumb and was taking up valuable space. I didn't even let myself imagine a graduation goal.

I walked the campus until I found each of my classrooms

for my first semester in the days before school started. I asked every administrator I spoke with where I could find a school job. I spent hours in the college bookstore until I understood new books, used books, and, yes, blue books. During the first few days of classes, I realized that everyone, no matter her age, felt the same ignorance and trepidation.

I made that Journey successfully, as I did when I traveled to stay in a Buddhist monastery in Thailand, moved across the country from California to Indiana, changed careers when I was over forty, and made many more chosen Journeys. I've made the Hero's Journey before. So have you.

Here's how we can prove it:

Did you ever have a goal—something you felt strongly that you needed to do?

While you were working on this goal, did you experience something really bad or painful that waylaid you on the way?

While this bad thing was happening, did you have someone (or more than one person) who gave you advice to help you get through that rough phase?

Did you come out of that bad experience with new knowledge? Did that awful experience teach you a life lesson?

Would you be able to say that working toward that goal, and even those bad experiences, created a new "identity" for you? Did you find a new part of you? Maybe a new, stronger self?

After you reached your goal, did you share this information with at least one other person so they could benefit from what you learned?

That's the Hero's Journey.

You've done it at least once. You can do it again. And you can do it *on purpose.* You're on a Hero's Journey. Why not take control?

I think of my spiritual Journey to be the Hero's Journey that arcs my adult life. Within that arc are the spirals of many smaller-scale journeys, like writing this book

Look around you. Millions of people are on the Hero's Journey. Most people who complete a twelve-step program and stay abstinent have completed a Hero's Journey. Many people who become teachers did a Hero's Journey. When I finished and published my first book of poetry, I completed a Hero's Journey.

Human history is peppered with myths, legends, and news stories that reflect someone's Hero Journey. You know the big names: Beowulf, Odysseus, Luke Skywalker, Simba, Harry Potter. But do you know the stories of these phenomenal women: Boudicca, Penthesilea, Queen Nzingha, or Makeda, Queen of Sheba? Our culture emphasizes the male Hero story, and even I tend to think of these Heroes first.

As Joseph Campbell wrote in *The Hero with a Thousand Faces*, the Hero's Journey pattern is a part of our consciousness, whether it is expressed in a myth or in the Journey of a real person who suffered the physical pain and joy of venturing forth and returning home a changed person.

The Hero's Journey could be local, or it could be national or planetary. Ed Roberts advocated for his own wheelchair access while he attended school in Berkeley, California, and along the way knocked down barriers for millions of others. Aung San Suu Kyi was kept under house arrest for nearly fifteen years while she advocated for free elections and focused the world's attention on her country, Burma. Bill W. wanted to keep himself sober, and in the process created the first twelve-step program, Alcoholics Anonymous, which has saved the lives of millions since its founding in 1935.

7

Doing a single heroic act is not part of the Hero's Journey. Conversely, completing a Hero's Journey does not make you a Hero. It makes you a Wise One, one of the modern Magi. I believe you are on a Hero's Journey right now or you wouldn't be reading this.

Where are you on the spiral path that is the Hero's Journey?

Chapter 2. Where on the Hero's Journey Are You?

"If you don't know where you're going, you might not get there."—Yogi Berra

What's This Hero's Journey Stage About?

In classic stories, this stage is called the Ordinary World. This is the stage where you are walking around, living your normal life, but contemplating a new, audacious goal, although you haven't taken any action yet.

Have you ever truly been lost? I don't mean "Calle Vista street looks the same as Sierra Vista, which I can't tell from Luna Vista. . . ." By lost, I mean the kind of lost where you are in a park deep in the woods and there're no markings on what you think is still a trail and there's literally no other human around that you can hear or see. Or lost like the time you were driving that state route you thought went all the way through to Toledo, but now you're smack dab in the middle of farm fields as far as you can see on a road paved only one step up from gravel. Or lost like when you were seven and got separated from your family at the state fair and there were so many people and it was so very hot and the farm animal smell mixed with the cotton candy smell to make you want to throw up. It's not just your mind that starts to race—your body starts to react as if you are off balance or have vertigo. Your proprioceptors are sending panic messages to your brain, "Right the ship! Turn into the wind! Flaps up!"

My dad had a great sense of direction, probably honed from when roads had far less signage and travel took longer. He'd say, "Don't worry, we're still heading west." He'd also say,

"All roads lead to Rome," which he explained to mean that all roads connect *at some point*. You will meet a crossroads sooner or later, then you can orient yourself.

I frequently get lost in Chicago, because to me *the lake is not in the right place*. I grew up in Ohio, near Cleveland, where Lake Erie was always north of wherever I was. In Chicago, the lake—Lake Michigan—is always to the east. That's just wrong!

When you're lost, it's okay—in fact I encourage you— to say, "I don't know where I am." If you keep denying your lost-ness, you may only luck onto a direction, rather than move in the direction you desire. I find when I say that phrase out loud, like admitting, "I don't know," a magic happens that allows the direction to show up for me.

I got lost once deep in California's central valley. That region of California is almost all farms, stockyards, and brush. Somehow, I had gotten turned around off the state route, and all I could see was dirt and a couple of nodding oil jack-pumps. I felt like panicking, but instead I stopped the car, got out, and climbed to the top of a hill to see which way to go. Turned out, the right way was not at all the way I had been headed. Great advice comes from the poet David Wagoner, who wrote, "Stand still. The trees ahead and the bushes beside you are not lost."

Do you feel you're not where you're *supposed to be*? Most of that feeling comes from not having a guide, a map, or a reference point. This is where the map of the Hero's Journey stages will help you. You can see where you are on the map. You will see what's coming up next, and you'll have the tools to help you keep moving.

What You Believe Matters

Limiting beliefs impact the Journey aspect of our lives, too. Some people have felt bereft: "I was told to go this way. I was promised a fulfilling life if I went this way. At least, I thought I was promised that." Now maybe you know you are at a crossroads but not sure where that crossroads is, or which way those roads go. You don't know which turn to take.

You may notice clearly where others are on the Hero's Journey, but not yourself. I noticed it when Janet A., a friend of mine, told me she was going to become a certified yoga teacher. I remember saying to her, "You know that's a Hero's Journey, and you are right at the threshold."

She demurred. "I'm just going to yoga teacher training."

I responded, "Well, why isn't that a Hero's Journey? It's got a physical test. You have to pass the certification test at the end of it. You know this is new information for you, and you have to adjust your schedule and make a commitment. You will have a physical Trial. Once you learn all this new stuff, there will be information to pass on. That's the stage for the Road Back, where you bring the magic back to the village. That's a Hero's Journey."

"But I don't look like a yoga teacher . . . I'm too big . . . and I'm not a vegetarian," Janet said.

"Overcoming that—those ideas—is *exactly* what makes it a Hero's Journey," I told her.

"What do you mean?"

"Well, why are you doing this?"

"Since I moved so far away from family and the church I grew up in, it's all feeling topsy-turvy. There's a lot of freedom away from all that, and some anxiety. But I latched onto yoga because it's movement—joyful and deliberate movement. The teachers all have really positive messages, and when I leave class, I feel better. It makes me literally stretch and strengthen myself."

"But why go through teacher training?"

"When I found the Yoga of 12-step Recovery, which to me was like a thunderclap, like wow, what a great idea, these two things belong together. I was inspired by my teacher to get certified in order to be of service to those who mentored me, who gave me positive messages, who encouraged me. I wanted to do that in order to give back. It just was one of those things that seemed like I just had to do it, period."

"Like the Hero's Journey," I said.

Janet laughed. "Yes, like the Hero's Journey."

Maybe you are just curious what your life and adventures would look like if you thought of them as a Hero's Journey. When looked at from the viewpoint of the Journey, Janet's yoga teacher training was a bigger part of her life than she initially thought. When we change our idea of the things we do and realize how much we affect others, we see our activities in the light and magic of the Hero's Journey. Now her new skills are a part of her. Her Journey experiences are a part of her. We are all a part of a much bigger thing; we just forget sometimes.

The Hero's Journey Stages

The Hero's Journey has roughly twelve stages.

In the Regular World—Are you asleep under a picnic table in the park? Or climbing up a mountain? The regular world is your day-to-day life, with all of its joys and its stresses.

The Call to Adventure—You hear it; I know you hear it. It may be a quiet whisper or a banging gong or a high-def billboard on the side of the road. The Call is always to follow your bliss, and your bliss is defined completely by what *you* want.

Refusing the Call—This stage is so seductive: It's all

the excuses you make to not answer your Call. I'm not good enough, man enough, well dressed enough. I'm too busy. Let voicemail pick it up. I put my number on that do-not-call list. Call? What Call? I swear I never heard anything! Refusing the Call will definitely be an early stage, but it may also come back throughout your Journey.

Meeting the Mentor(s)—You cannot do this alone. You cannot even do a Journey by just reading this book. You must have a mentor. Your mentor/teacher is right there. Maybe you need to turn around to see her. You will likely have more than one mentor on the Journey. You will also have allies who help you along the Journey in many different ways. The magic of synchronicity for finding and having mentors and allies is that you are as necessary to them as they are to you to complete the Journey.

Crossing the Threshold—You decide to do it. This is the stage where you step across that threshold and make the first step on your Adventure. At first you feel the threshold is a force field; an inuksuk, a barrier, a climb over a fence. This is where your first step takes you over the moat, then you turn back and see the barrier was an illusion. But you can't see that it was an illusion until you take a step over the threshold. Once over it, you meet a Guardian of the threshold whose job it is to confirm your commitment to your Journey.

Tests and Trials—Really? Another Test?? There will be a few, or maybe more than a few, as you build up your physical, emotional, and spiritual muscles to keep moving through the stages. Getting through this stage makes you ready for the next ones.

The Approach—This is where you see the reward, the grail, the mountains in the distance, and you're so, so close . . . and the way you're used to doing things isn't working. How can I change my approach?

Ordeal and a Death—This is the true reckoning of the Hero's Journey. Someone, or something, will die on this stage. It could be physical, emotional, or spiritual, or all three at once. Here, you go through the ultimate Test for this Journey.

Reward—You seize the magic. You feel it—Awe!!! It fills you up, and it was all worth it, every Trial. Every pain was worth it just for this feeling! You have a level of knowledge and awareness you didn't think possible before you started the Journey.

The Road Back—Arghhh! This road is long. Was it this long going up the mountain?? And now I have to drag the magic back down, over hill and dale. Do I want to go back to the regular world? Can't I just stay here with my accomplishment?

Resurrection—What died before is born anew and better. The old you that started this Journey doesn't exist anymore, and you reach atonement with yourself and others. What resurrects are your lost parts of your self. It doesn't make the Ordeal any easier . . .

Return to the Village with the Magic—You share what you have learned with others. Maybe you start a new Journey. You may become a mentor to others.

Here is a real-life example of the stages of the Journey:

Janet was enjoying her yoga classes, attending regularly **(Ordinary World)**. She attended a different class one day, Yoga for 12-Step Recovery (Y12SR) and felt the Call to teach this type of yoga class, "like a thunderclap" **(Call to Adventure).** Janet thought about the commitment of several months with no free weekends. She cringed at being in front of the other teachers, who she thought all would be younger and have perfect yoga bodies **(Refusing the Call).**

Kim, the instructor of the Y12SR class she took, encouraged her directly and by her courageous behavior while teaching. "Kim was not afraid to get down there intimately with people, touch them, adjust them, over their protestations that they don't want to do it or they can't. She makes them do it, which I think is tremendously courageous" **(Meeting the Mentor).**

Even though she had some resistance, Janet took the first step and signed up for the certification classes. Her teacher for certification was "a little bit of a yoga tyrant, she didn't put up with any guff. She was also very, very tiny and very skinny. She just kind of had that look in her eye like, are you going to do this? At that moment, I realized that if the process was going to work, or if I was going to get anywhere, and if I was paying to get better, then I ought to do what she said" **(Crossing the Threshold).**

Week after week, nearly the entire weekend was taken up with hours-long classes, studying material, and pushing herself into literally new shapes. For Janet, the certification training itself was hard to do and a little bit scary. "I felt out of place there with the other women, but I was determined. I kept telling myself that I am going to do this" **(Tests and Trials).**

There were times when Janet's boyfriend, Mike, was cheering her along the path: "Don't give up, don't skip class, don't do that." She said, "Well, other people are doing it." Mike responded, "So what? That's their problem. You're not them." Janet had to do service tasks like sweeping the studios, checking in students, and cleaning restrooms. She realized she had to look at these tasks differently. She couldn't measure her own achievement by comparison to anyone, even her own expectations **(The Approach).**

As the weekend of the certification test approached, Janet's father was hospitalized and in serious condition. She had to make a hard decision about what to do. Family in Chicago were calling, "You have to come now." But Janet decided to stay through the weekend and she finished the certification test successfully. Her joy was tempered by her father's death a few weeks later **(The Ordeal and the Reward).**

Janet is grieving the loss of her father and struggling not to see herself as an orphan, now that her mother and father are both gone. With the loss, she realized that her father had handed new responsibilities to her. "Knowledge that now I need to pass on to the village: my sons, my friends, my family. I need to be available and pass on what I have learned about love. And mostly the idea—I will never forget this one—Kim, when I came into my first Y12SR class, had a little sign that said, 'You are kind of a big deal.' I almost broke into tears when I read that. That's the message that I have to pass on. Yes, you are a big deal" **(The Road Back and the Resurrection).**

Janet teaches Y12SR classes twice a month to bring what she's learned "back to the tribe." She also fills in for her first mentor, Kim. Janet admits she hasn't yet fully realized her goal to set up her own Y12SR classes, but she is more patient with herself and her goals now **(Return to the Village with the Magic).**

Exercise: Find Your Place on the Map

You might be at the start of the Journey. Maybe you just decided today to do a Hero's Journey (yea for you!!). Are you flitting around like a hummingbird? Or trudging along a dusty road with nothing but a roll of hills as far as you can see?

You might be right in the middle of the Journey. You might be in the stage I think is the most difficult: the Road Back. It doesn't matter. Once you identify where you are, you can pack appropriately, get out your map, and set out to move further along. Take control wherever you are in the Journey.

Most stages of the Journey blend together and overlap, with really squidgy edges. Some stages go very quickly, and some go on for what seems like ages. They each have their appropriate length of time, unless you've just given up, fallen into a pothole, or been set upon by a Highwayman.

What do you need to do today to keep moving on y our Hero's Journey?

Your task for today is to look at the map and read through the twelve stages to identify what stage you're in. Take your finger and put yourself on the spiral map of the Hero's Journey. See! That was easy.

Chapter 3. Who's Calling? Your Adventure!

> *"Life is a Journey that must be traveled no matter how bad the roads and accommodations."—Oliver Goldsmith*

What's This Hero's Journey Stage About?

Ah! This is the Hero's Journey stage where you admit you are hearing a Call for a great goal, a big change, or a daring quest. It is the Call to Adventure!

You hear it.

You know you hear it.

I know you hear it.

Your best friend knows you hear it. She's heard you talk about what you want to do many times.

Campbell named the initial stage of the Journey a "Call to Adventure." It may be a whisper or a banging gong or a billboard on the side of the road. For me it sounded like the nagging buzz of a mosquito. For others, the Call is as loud as a claxon and as obvious as sky-writing. It feels like an itch you just have to scratch. It is the Call to "follow your bliss." What will make you truly satisfied?

In a 90s movie, *Fools Rush In,* actors Matthew Perry and Salma Hayek played a romantic couple on the edge of break-up. Separated across the country from her, he starts seeing signs that direct him back to Salma's character, his true love.

He sees the Grand Canyon on a Times Square billboard,

encounters little dark-eyed girl with the same name as his partner, and a mumbling man on a New York street who tells him there are signs everywhere.

We aren't all fortunate enough to have our Call be that blatant.

More likely, the Call is a feeling, a whim . . . a nudge toward a *you* that feels more real than what you are living now.

Your Call may be as simple as, "I want to do that." Whatever "that" is.

Your Call and your Adventure are unique to you.

More and more scientific evidence tells us how intelligent the feelings in our bodies are—and to listen to those messages. Organs attached to the vagus nerve are our body's nonverbal communication system. Messages travel along this wire, bypassing our analytical thinking engine and go directly to the action part of the brain, directly from the gut and the heart.

Using this Call—the one only you can hear—is the surest way to initiate your own Hero's Journey. If you listen to this Call and respond, I guarantee you a Journey of integrity. If you attempt to make your Journey on what others think you should be doing (parents, friends, teachers, etc.) it will likely never feel quite right to you and the Trials will not feel worth the effort. The Journey must always be what *you* want to achieve.

Two years ago, I sat reading the book *Ruby*, by Cynthia Bond. It was late in the evening, and I was slouched down in my "big chair" with my legs bent over the chair arm. In the story, Ruby, is in the woods and meets the crone, Ma Tante, who grabs her hand and points, "You got da mystic star. There." I turned my own head and looked at my hand holding the book, backlit by a small table lamp. The star shape lined out on my own hand was as clear as if I had drawn it with a Sharpie.

A part of me wondered why I had never seen this shape even after fifty years of looking at my own hands. The other part knew I just didn't want to see it. Regardless of the significance I placed on the lines on my hand, I knew they meant I should stop denying my shamanic gifts and help others.

It has taken me several decades to accept the Call and trust my own voice. I will differentiate here—when I say "my own voice," I mean the deep, quiet knowing voice—my intuition, not the critic. Not the fear-based version of the critic either—the protector. After those voices are quieted—and it takes a while—then I can hear my true voice. I know it as my true voice by how I feel when I listen to it: calm, sure, safe, and loved. The sign was there, as clear and plain as the nose on my face. Or the lines on my hand.

Maybe your sign will not be as clearly outlined as mine was. I had plenty of signs before that evening. I didn't ignore them, but I let them only inch me along my Journey.

My signs were always body-centric; that is, they were about how my body felt—like Janet describing her feeling of knowing as "landing." Jana L. says she hears a voice saying something short and distinct," but the range of my attention is wide then, it's like a big globe around my head, shoulders and heart. I feel assured. Discussion ended, I KNOW." Sylvia B. describes her intuition as a warm and connected feeling that radiates from her heart to lower in her body.

My intuition knows when I understand in my head, and the feelings in my body sing back in harmony.

Listening to the voice of my intuition doesn't negate fear or anxiety, but whenever I listen to my true voice I am better equipped to ignore, have compassion for, and even laugh at the critical voices in my head. As my friend and author, Claudia S. says, "Don't believe all of what you think."

BERNADETTE SOUBIROUS

In the 1943 movie, *The Song of Bernadette*, Jennifer Jones won an Academy Award for her portrayal of the teenager, Bernadette Soubirous. I attended Catholic school in the 1960s. I saw this movie and, like most who saw it, was moved by the girl who stood by her story in the face of ridicule, ostracism, and accusations of insanity. I believe the real Bernadette Soubirous believed she experienced visions of a beautiful Lady who directed her to dig up a spring and build a chapel on the spot where she saw her. Did she know this spring and chapel would turn into the pilgrimage destination Lourdes we know today? No—and it didn't matter to her. Her Call was to do as the Lady directed.

Most important to the Call is that you believe you hear it and know what it means to you. *No one else's opinion matters.* You know your Call has a purpose for others, but it also has a purpose for you.

In the Hero's Journey, the "Call" is a Call to Adventure. My *Webster's New Twentieth Century Dictionary* defines *adventure* as "a bold undertaking in which hazards are to be encountered and the issue is staked upon unforeseen events," and "a remarkable occurrence in one's personal history."

What is your Call to Adventure?

What are you hearing?

Is it a Call to live more simply?

A Call to build a school?

A Call to solve your child's allergy suffering?

A Call to hike the Appalachian Trail?

Are you hearing a Call to change your career to one that helps and serves others more than you do now?

Do you just want to learn the play the drums?

I know many people who hear a Call unique to themselves. Sherry H., an IT Project Manager, knew she had to build a school in the Ethiopian village she visited. Sylvia B. became a Patient Advocate to help others navigate the healthcare system while they were in the chaos of a frightening diagnosis, as she had learned during her own cancer treatment. Maria M. knew she could turn the old-time management world on its head and help graduate students complete their dissertations.

Exercise: Listening to Your Body for the Call

Here is a way to test for your Call to Adventure:

1. Make a short list of three big things you'd like to accomplish. Just write them down on a piece of paper, numbered 1, 2, 3. These list items should be anything you'd really, really like to achieve. *This is not a grocery list.*

2. Sit quietly and imagine yourself starting on your Journey toward that first goal listed.

3. As you imagine yourself moving toward that first goal, responding to the Call, take notice of how your body feels.

4. Jot a couple of words down to describe that feeling

in your body.

5.   Repeat this for all three items.

Let's look at what you noted for your body's reaction.

Did your body relax, or did you feel your throat constrict?

How about your breathing? Was it more rapid, or calm and relaxed?

Did you hear a rush in your ears?

Do you want to stop imagining?

Do you want to turn back?

Are you feeling sensations you can only describe as anxiety or fear?

Did you imagine yourself whistling and skipping down the yellow brick road? Dancing, splashing, and singing in the rain? If you did, *that is not your Hero's Journey*.

When I did this exercise with Claudia S., a corporate trainer and author, she was confused. "I thought I would feel excited and eager to begin. This is a Hero's Journey, after all. But all I want to do is get up and run in the other direction."

I told her that not only was her fear normal, but it was a clear marker that her Call was a Hero's Journey.

Are you confused? Did you think you would feel giggly shivers of joy starting out on your Hero's Journey? Ha! Your fear is the best indicator that you are on the right track.

Why is that?

Remember that you will move out of the Ordinary World once you decide to begin your Journey. The Ordinary World is comfortable. The Ordinary World has recliner chairs,

23

the TV remote, and romance novels. These are not scary things because they are so well known.

What is unknown is scary—and it's scary to all humans. It's built into our brains and bodies to fear what we don't know and aren't accustomed to. It's how our ancestors survived to create us!

The magical world that your Call to Adventure will bring is unknown to you. You just feel that you have to follow the Call. You have to do it. Or at least, you have to try.

If you're hearing a few calls, you may be wondering how you can sift through the noise of the various desires. Do this exercise with each one.

The one item on your list you are most afraid of is your Hero's Journey for *right now*. You've heard the Call, but you are slipping into the next stage—you've refused the Call.

On Purpose

You don't have to wait for fate to throw you onto a Hero's Journey. There is plenty of precedent for going on your Hero's Journey *on purpose*. Many indigenous cultures have traditions where initiations or vision quests are self-initiated. In traditional Lakota culture, when an older child is ready, he or she will go on a personal or spiritual quest alone—a *hanblecheyapi* (literally, "crying for a vision"). Among First Nations people of Canada, adolescents must undertake the vision quest to be accepted as adults in the community. "Walkabout" refers to a rite of passage during which indigenous adolescent male Australians undergo a Journey, typically between ages 10 and 16. They must live in the wilderness for a period as long as six months to make the spiritual and traditional transition into manhood.

Every time you decide to make a change to yourself and your life, every time you set an audacious goal for yourself, you are setting out on a Hero's Journey on purpose. You have taken control of the Journey deliberately.

What do you need to do today to keep moving on your Hero's Journey?

This will be hard for some of you. Find a big sticky note or get a piece of paper. Write down a few lines to describe your Hero's Journey Call/Quest/Adventure. Don't get all panicky that it has to be perfect. Your Hero's Journey will refine itself as you move along.

Seriously, get up right now and do it.

Chapter 4. Accept the Call and Stop Refusing the Journey

"We meet our destiny on the road we take to avoid it."—Carl Jung

What's This Hero's Journey Stage About?

The stage called Refusing the Call varies in length depending upon your commitment to avoiding your Call. It's ironic that you *say* you want to do this, but you never quite get around to it. Once you stop refusing your mission, the universe will line up help for you!

I refused the Call for years. I even yelled back at it to shut up.

Even today, when I have said out loud, "I am Shaman. I am part of a family of guides, teachers, and healers," self-doubt pops up. I know I am (as of this writing) in the final stage of that Journey, where I am bringing the magic back to the village. I'm living my message. I am sharing it. Then uncertainty shows up again: I don't look like a shaman. I wasn't raised to believe in this role. I have no legacy to fall back on. It's like an infectious case of déjà vu. I've been here before, I know. I thought I faced this and dealt with it. It's back *again*?

Some people hear the Call, "Yeah, I hear you, but I could never do that. I'm not [insert your favorite inadequacy here] enough." I know self-doubt shows up for me still because "I don't look right." A friend gave me an assignment to find ten examples of practicing shamans who don't look like Native Americans or Mayans (which is how I thought a shaman had to look). I made a PowerPoint slide with their pictures and webpage links to prove it to myself, yet the voice of "not quite right" still sometimes whispers to me.

When you are initiating a Hero's Journey, you identify the Call yourself. The part of Refusing the Call is played by the negative voices in your head. Some people turn up the music, the to-do list, or the substance distraction (alcohol, shopping, food, drugs) to twelve on the dial, just so they can drown out the Call. They point to all of their obligations: work, family, the garage needs cleaning, the kids need a ride to soccer practice.

The trouble with the Call is it never stops until you answer it.

It can get quieter, but it *never, ever* stops.

Well, now is the time to turn off the refusals, sit down, and really listen to the Call.

The first excuse is built on what somebody told you or you just inferred about the Hero's Journey. You may tell yourself, or someone else will tell you, that a Hero's Journey is:

- A myth—it's only in books or movies
- Needs a grand—even planetary—backdrop
- Is part of a war
- Requires a weapon: sword, light saber, Paul Bunyan-sized ax, magic wand
- For men only
- For large men only
- For white people only
- For adults only
- Not a part of your regular job
- Only for vibrantly healthy people
- Involves hundreds, if not thousands, of people
- Must be all about saving humanity or maybe the planet

This is all baloney.

Can a woman go on a Hero's Journey?

Can a child?

Can anyone who is not a tall, muscled, white man?

I say, yes—a resounding yes. Age, complexion, gender, shoe size, education, and sword-swinging ability are not relevant.

In his book, *The Adventure Gap*, James Edwards Mills, an African-American journalist, writes that even the publications he worked for showed hikers and climbers as "square-jawed white men with blond hair and blue eyes." He wrote *The Adventure Gap* to tell the stories of people of color, like him, who loved being out in nature and are active climbers and mountaineers. He says that he has never felt unwelcome or out of place with his colleagues and fellow adventurers, but he also "can't help but wonder, 'Where are all the black folks?'"

Maureen Murdock, author of *The Heroine's Journey*, wrote that she interviewed Joseph Campbell, the definer of the Hero's Journey and its stages, and asked him about a woman making the Hero's Journey. Murdock wrote, *"I was surprised when he responded that women don't need to make the Journey."*

My eyes filled with tears reading this. If Campbell had still been alive, I would have gone to great lengths to contact him. I was so hurt and angry and felt so misunderstood. How could such an insightful thinker have gotten this one thing so terribly wrong? My reaction was part of what fueled me to write this. Was his response due to a sexist, limited view of women? Was it a result of his age? Or did he believe that women were exempt from the Hero's Journey because, as he said to Murdock, "All she has to do is to realize that she's the place that people [sic] are trying to get to. When a woman realizes what her wonderful character is, she's not going to get messed up with the notion of being pseudo-male."

I believe he was a victim of the sexism of his age and the limitations of those beliefs—even the beliefs that appear to put women on a pedestal. I sure wish I could talk to him today!

Plenty of people around you will help you resist your calling. Parents will warn you there's no money in it. Friends don't understand why you can't party with them anymore. The media will make you think your body isn't right for the job.

Even those brought up in cultures with strong traditions of callings can resist. The Xhosa people believe that *ukuthwasa* is a "healing sickness." Ukuthwasa is a period of initiation to become a traditional healer. Families regard it as both a gift from the ancestors and a burden. Training and treatment involves the new healer and his or her relatives in a long, demanding, and expensive process. When someone is thought to be in ukuthwasa, families will resist and deny the calling, asking many other practitioners and healers to negate the ukuthwasa.

Sometimes it's just us, though. Everything aligns to help us along our way, and yet we dither. Heather P. was working as a research assistant and completed all the required steps to return to graduate school for her advanced degree. Her family supplied her with some financial support, she had been accepted to the program she desired, yet she still resisted taking the final step. One day a friend told her, *"Heather, if you don't do your PhD, it is your choice now—you are clearly the one saying 'No.'"*

ACHILLES

In Homer's epic poem, *The Iliad*, Achilles, the quintessential warrior archetype, refused his Call

29

more than once.

His first refusal is when Odysseus shows up to tell him of Agamemnon's Call to fight against the Trojans.

Achilles' second refusal occurred while he was languishing in his tent refusing to fight, and his friend Patroclus was killed. Patroclus had donned Achilles' armor and sneaked out into the fight, where the Trojan prince Hector—thinking he was Achilles—killed him.

Later, after Odysseus said to Achilles, "You were the greatest, so fortunate in life that surely death must not pain you so much. Achilles responded, "Let me hear no smooth talk of death from you, Odysseus, light of councils. Better, I say, to break sod as a farm hand for some poor country man, or iron rations, then lord it over all the exhausted dead."

In this final comment, Achilles showed he is disillusioned by the idea of glory and weary of his warrior role and the death he has caused. He died in battle before the Trojan War ended.

Though a great warrior and still lauded thousands of years later, Achilles never completed a Hero's Journey. A Hero's Journey requires completing the stages of Resurrection, the Road Back and Bringing the Magic back to the Village. The main character may die metaphorically or even literally on the Hero's

Journey, but must be Resurrected in *some form* in order to complete the final stages and take the Journey full circle. That form can be spirit or legacy (passed onto a child, for example) but it must exist. The Hero must complete the final stages. Whether out of petulance, self-pity, or anger (or all of those), whether it was his emotions or his fate, Achilles made choices that turned him away from completing the Hero's Journey. How different the story of the Iliad would be had Achilles stopped fighting and brought this message to his brethren!

Exercise: It's a Wonderful Life

In the movie, *It's a Wonderful Life,* George gets upset and angry one terrible night. Standing on a bridge in the snow, he contemplates jumping. Clarence, an almost angel, jumps from the bridge, prompting George to rescue him from the frigid water. Later, when they're both drying off in the bridge-keeper's shack, George says, "I wish I'd never been born." Uh-oh! Clarence grants his wish (Be careful what you wish for!) then sets out to show him how the lives of the people in George's town would be if, as he wished, he'd never been there.

Try this short exercise to illustrate why your message (or even your example of following the Call to go on a Hero's Journey) needs to get out to others, and why you need to stop Refusing the Call, whatever your reasons.

1. At the top of your page write "It's a Wonderful Life."

2. Under that, write the words "my message," and after, that write your message. Your message is why you are on the Hero's Journey. It is your purpose for the Journey, your calling and goal. It's the nagging message you clarified in the previous chapter. Stop waffling like Achilles did in the *Iliad.* You know what it is. One example might be Gwen C.'s message. Gwen is an elementary school teacher. Her

31

message is: "We are all supremely powerful if we tap into the forces within. Life is to be lived and can only be achieved if you get hold of it, rather than allowing it to get hold of you."

3. Leave about three lines of empty space on the page.

4. Under the space, list three or more people to whom you have told your message. These are people who hear you espouse your opinions. They hear you go on about it and rarely stop you. They may even agree and contribute to the conversation. Put each name on one line or leave space between the names if your paper isn't lined.

5. Draw a vertical line down the page so each name has two columns after the empty space.

6. Now go back up to the space you left, under where you wrote "My Message" and write "My Anti-Message." In that space, write down the most polar opposite message you can think of to your message. This is the message people like those on your list above may hear if you're not around—if you don't follow your "Call" and don't complete your Hero's Journey (Like George in the movie!). Make sure that message is extreme and exaggerated even if it makes you feel uncomfortable to write the anti-message.

It's a Wonderful Life!
My goal—my message:

My anti-message:	
Names of people who know about my goal or have heard:	
1.	
2.	
3.	

Gwen listed:

Jennifer

Rick

Olivia

Gwen's anti-message: We are all pathetic, weak, and frightened beings. We are at the mercy of all the monsters around us all the time. Life is to be cowered in, as the monsters

33

poke, punch, and strangle the joy out of you.

7. Go down to each name on your list, and after each name, write how that person's life will turn out if they hear only the anti-message. As if you were never around. As if you'd never been born.

8. After you write an anti-message for each person, think about how each person's life will turn out if they hear and act on your real message.

When she's completed the exercise, Gwen's sheet looks like:

It's a Wonderful Life!		
My goal—my message: *We are all supremely powerful if we tap into the forces within. Life is to be lived and can only be achieved if you get hold of it, rather than allowing it to get hold of you.*		
My anti-message: *We are all pathetic, weak, and frightened beings. We are at the mercy of all the monsters around us all the time. Life is to be cowered in as the monsters poke, punch, and strangle the joy out of you.*		
Jennifer	Never finishes school and moves down into the basement of her parents' house	Creates a blog for her comics and posts weekly. She adds advertising to her site and creates

	because she was too afraid to talk to any girl she likes. She works in a toll booth during the day and draws cartoon aliens on her bedroom walls at night, wishing they would come and take her away.	enough passive income to return to school to finish her degree.
Rick	Works in a job where he answers a customer service line that no one ever calls. He is not allowed to read or do puzzles while he waits for calls. He spends the day clicking his mouse on the four corners of his screen.	Rick decides to ignore the critical voices from his family and in his head and begins taking classes to become a massage therapist.
Olivia	Olivia says she loves to learn. She signs up for new classes at the local college annex often. She just goes to the first one, which is enough to remind her that she's stupid and will never be able to do the course work. She can't stand to be	Olivia gets a friend to sign up with her for a class and sit close to her and help her stay. Olivia likes bringing a friend to class so much she starts a service to connect class-buddies for adult students.

	humiliated like that, so she never goes back.	

When we completed the exercise, Gwen complained, "I wish Jennifer would actually listen to me. She could be so much further ahead. It's like she doesn't hear me at all. Or she disagrees with me and just won't tell me."

I asked Gwen, "Is she as bad off as what you wrote for her life in your anti-message?"

"Well, no. But she could be so great. She's really an amazing artist. She thinks of things I never could," Gwen said.

"Maybe she does hear," I suggested, "and her life and her pace really are a reflection of hearing you and your encouragement. You just want her to move at your pace, and she has her own."

Most of us refuse the Call because we know we are leaving safety—physical, psychic, emotional, and spiritual. It's no small thing to do what makes you blissfully happy, and it ripples out in many ways and all around you. You must learn that you can trust what you love more than you fear what you fear. Let's read that sentence again: *You must learn that you can trust what you love more than you fear what you fear.*

Will it be worth it? Let's see.

What do you need to do today to keep moving on your Hero's Journey?

First, do the exercise. The exercise will help you see that you *do* make an impact and your unique voice *does* make a difference in the world.

Second, commit to yourself that you will just do the next step. You don't have to go beyond that. Just the next step. So, turn the page already!

Chapter 5. Mentor and Allies: Build your Team

"The best teachers are those who show you where to look, but don't tell you what to see."—
Alexandra K. Trenfor

What's This Hero's Journey Stage About?

The Mentors and Allies stage is when you build your team to help and accompany you on your Hero's Journey. You make friends! You learn new things! You get help all along the way. It's just as easy as it sounds.

You cannot go on a Hero's Journey alone. You just can't. You may think you're alone, but you're not. On your Journey, you will have Mentors and Allies, along with some not-so-helpful folks. Let's start with the obvious one—the mentor.

The dictionary defines a mentor as 1) a wise and trusted counselor or teacher, and 2) an influential senior sponsor or supporter.

The key words are wise and trusted. A mentor could be someone who is just a little bit further along the path than you. A mentor would say, "As you come around that curve, be careful; the rocks are loose there, so stay close to the wall." A mentor cares about you, gives you good advice, and teaches you ways to navigate the rougher parts of the Journey, when she can't always be at your side.

You will have a mentor—maybe several mentors—each at different points on your Journey. The mentor who gets you started is unlikely to be the one who drags you back to the village and over the finish line. To have a mentor, you must first overcome any idea you have that "I should know how to do this." Funny, some of us think that for everything we try!

Mentor relationships are necessary throughout your life. My first mentor was Gene Dulmage, my high school speech and drama teacher. He set high standards for teenagers. He assigned us classic Greek and contemporary plays to read. He expected us to understand what we read, interpreted, and performed-- and we did. I know I still love live theater because of his influence.

My first spiritual mentor was Devon Crane., a teacher who started me on my formal spiritual path. When I speak with him today, he always says something that rocks me back on my heels and makes me think differently. The angle from which he looks at life is so different from mine. He provokes and prods me even after twenty years.

In *The Iliad*, Mentor was Odysseus' friend. Odysseus trusted him to care for his home and family when he left for Troy. Was Mentor a real person? Did he really live? Maybe. Maybe not. But his name became an important word in our language.

How do you come to trust your mentor? One way is to acknowledge her experience and point of view as valuable. Accept her good intentions for you and your Journey. Your trust leads to recognition of her wisdom, which gains more trust, which moves you both further up in consciousness.

Another key word in the mentor definition is sponsor or supporter. Your mentor at each point of your Journey supports you—steadies you when you wobble or falter and turns you around when you're headed in the wrong direction. In a twelve-step program, your sponsor is there for you when you call near a breaking point. Your mentor listens and responds to your questions.

Goddess Athene

Rare for classical literature, it is a female, the Goddess Athene, who is the archetypal mentor in *The Odyssey*, helping Odysseus, his son Telemachus, and others many times.

Disguised as Odysseus friend Mentor, so Telemachus would trust her advice, Athene goes to Odysseus' house and advises Telemachus to find information about his father.

As Odysseus gets closer to his home, some of the other gods use their powers against him. When the sea god, Poseidon, sends a storm to delay Odysseus on his raft, Athene intervenes and calms the winds and drifts Odysseus to where he will find help from the Phaeacian people.

When Odysseus washes up on the beach of Phaecia, Athene plays up Odysseus' masculine attributes, to cause the Princess Nausicaa to be attracted to the Greek Hero and provide him more than she would if he looked like a scrawny, ugly guy.

Athene disguises herself as a little Phaeacian girl and leads Odysseus toward the king's

palace while she tells him the history of
Phaeacia, so he is prepared to speak with the
king when he pleas for help to get home.

Once Odysseus is conveyed back home to
Ithaca and is left sleeping on the shore, Athene
hides him in a protective cloud so nobody can
see him or his treasure as he sleeps.

How great it must have been to have such a powerful
and creative mentor as Athene!

So maybe you don't have the Goddess Athene for a
mentor, but let's identify the mentors you do have right now.

Number one, you have me, the author. I'm telling you
my experiences and what I have learned from my own Journeys,
so you can navigate yours more easily. I want you to achieve
your bliss. I want you to get through your Journey and bring
your magic back to the village.

Who else brought you to this point?

How does she support you?

In what ways is she wise?

How do you know you can depend on her advice?

Think back to the definition of a mentor: 1) A wise and
trusted counselor or teacher, and 2) an influential senior sponsor
or supporter. Does it say anywhere there what the mentor must
look or sound like? Does it say that the mentor must be an old
white dude? Old? White? Dude?

You have to shake up your idea of what the mentor
archetype (an idealized or typical example) is. *Star War's* Obi-
Wan will not be everyone's mentor. Remember when Luke

Skywalker said he was looking for a great Jedi Master to teach him? Yoda (small, green . . .) was not what Luke thought a Jedi Master would look like.

One of your mentors may not be human. In the original Pinocchio story, one of his mentors is a talking cricket and another is a fairy. In the American folk tale, Paul Bunyan is accompanied in his work by a giant blue ox, Babe. Just like at different points on your Journey, you may have different mentors. Your mentors may take different, even noncorporeal shapes. Your mentor may be an animal, a spirit, a supernatural being, a symbol or a sign.

One week, hawks were stalking me. Three times in as many days I noticed one perched near me. I asked myself what a hawk meant to me. Certainly, a hawk is a hunter and has keen eyesight. Some consider the hawk to be a messenger omen or spirit animal. I took the presence of the hawks in a different way. Hawks use the thermal layers in the air to float and glide while they are hunting, conserving energy. These hawks reminded me to be patient—to float on the currents around me—while changes come to fruition. I tend to be impatient and can use a lot of reminders. With practice, I am learning to notice the teachers and mentors that surround me every day.

WHERE THE TWO CAME TO THEIR FATHER

In the Navaho Warrior Initiation, Where the Two Came to Their Father, the twin boys, Nayainazgana (Slayer of Alien Gods) and Tobadzaschaina (Born from Water), meet Spider Woman, who gives the two boys a feather to protect them as they move through the obstacles on their way to the ocean that surrounds the world. When they reach the edge of the ocean, they hold the feather between them and use its magical protective power to cross the ocean and reach the home of their father—the Sun.

As you gather and choose mentors on the different stages of your Journey, a word of caution. There may be times when your mentor does not appear to have your best interest at heart. She may have your Journey's best outcome at heart. It may take a while for you to see that.

One example of this kind of mentor is a serious disease or illness, like multiple sclerosis or cancer. You could look at your disease as part of the Tests and Trials stage, but I think it is more useful and powerful to see that it functions more like a mentor. A disease will force you to do things you would not otherwise choose to do. A disease will show you aspects of yourself you never had to look at before. A disease will drag you to the edge of the abyss, knowing you would never intentionally walk there.

Sylvia B., has become an insurance expert so she can help others when they find out they have cancer. Sylvia had two bouts with cancer in the last several years. "I know my life would be completely different if I had never gotten cancer, or even if I decided to react differently when I found out. I hated, *hated* my cancer the first time around. It was a monster that had to be obliterated. The second time I found out, I thought, "Why me? I swear I heard a voice that said, "Well, why not you?" After some whining and crying I decide that cancer does not know who it's messin' with! That's when I let it guide me to my new life and career. As weird as that sounds."

Allies on Your Journey

Where the mentor sometimes teaches you harshly, allies

will always be on your side. Like mentors, allies might not be human or even corporeal, so keep your eyes and your options open. You're creating a team to keep you on track for your Journey's goal.

Keep allies around you. You become more productive when surrounded and supported by allies. Allies create the magic of synergy, where the results are greater than the sum of each person's individual effect. If you listen to your intuition, you will not only find more allies, your intuition may tell you to open up about your Journey with a new friend or colleague. You can rely on ally input to help you resolve problems and even delegate activities. Conversely, your intuition may tell you that some of your friends or family may not be ready to hear about your Journey quite yet. Trust the feeling messages of your intuition.

One of my current allies is Gregory Ferger, my body worker and massage therapist. Most of the time, I just tell Gregory what's going on in my life or what I would like to know more about, and he does the rest. My eyes are usually closed and I'm under a sheet. I trust him. I don't know what he does, and really, that's his job, not mine. I consistently experience amazing visions and spiritual journeying with his assistance. He always greets me like I am the most interesting person he's ever met. Making me feel special is the mark of a true ally.

An ally like a Higher Power, a core concept of all twelve-step programs (and most people's lives), can be called upon for guidance at any hour. All of my fellow twelve-step program members make good allies because they are very good at listening. Sometimes you don't need help fixing a problem. You just need an ear to listen and a shoulder to lean on.

What looks like a friend may fight against you on the Journey. You will have to remind yourself that everyone has her own Journey. In the story, *An Echo Through the Snow*, Rosalie's boyfriend scoffs at her idea of taking night classes to become a veterinary technician before he stomps off into the night. A

44

person she loves and expects to support her denigrates and abandons her. Like this story's character, you may run up against resistance from people you called friends who cannot be an ally on your Journey. For whatever reason, they don't want you to complete your Journey. It's sad to learn this, but you don't have to discount them as friends, just remember they have a different role on your Hero's Journey.

Take a **Rest Stop** right here and do an inventory of your team: your Mentors and Allies. As you review each of them, note what each brings to you that no one else does. Create the feeling of appreciation for each Mentor and Ally, and say thank you out loud for each one.

You can do a lot of cool things in your life, but these accomplishments will not be a Hero's Journey if you don't have mentors, allies, and helpers. Part of the Hero's Journey is the experience that you have as a human being *with other human beings*. Your human experience is what keeps the Hero's Journey a part of consciousness—part of all of us.

Exercise: What Is a Mentor?

Some mentors are nonhuman. Limiting our helpers to humans is short-sighted. Sometimes on the Hero's Journey we need a mentor who can go where humans can't, or see and hear what humans can't.

On a blank piece of paper, draw and number three lines.

On line number one, please write the name of an animal that comes to mind. Don't filter or edit it, just write it down. For some people, the first answer that pops into their head feels the best. For others, more thought is required.

On line number two, please write down the name of a natural element or natural thing. Whatever comes to mind is the right response. Just write it down.

45

On the line numbered three, please write the name of a supernatural or noncorporeal (doesn't have a body) being that comes to mind. Again, don't filter or edit your thoughts, just write the name down.

Now here is the fascinatingly fun part—which will all take place in your imagination.

Imagine that you show up on your first day of a class to learn more about how to complete your Journey and answer your Call. The professor turns out to be the most shocking surprise!!

1. You listen raptly to a lecture from Professor [your response number one]. You are amazed at what Professor [same animal] is teaching you. What did Professor [number one again] tell you about your Journey that you didn't know before?

Gwen C., the elementary school teacher, did this exercise and listed:

1. Meerkat
2. The ocean
3. Grandmother's spirit (maybe an angel)

For her response to number one, Gwen C. wrote:

The meerkat told me to stand up. It was so simple. I laughed, because I could see them all standing up looking around on the savannah. My message to people that we are all powerful if we tap into the forces within *requires* me to stand up. Stand up for myself and stand up for others who need my help, and stand up to voices that want to hold us down. You have better leverage if you are standing up!

2. On this imaginary course, you have a lecture and lab practical. Professor [your response number two, some element or natural thing] has you learning things about your Journey you never imagined. What practical exercises does Professor [natural

46

element or thing] use to teach?

Gwen C. wrote for response number two:

At first, it seemed like the ocean had nothing to tell me. I just remembered being on a beach one time during vacation. I remembered the smell and the feel of the sand and water on my feet. Then a strange thing happened, I heard a voice that said, 'Get outside.' That's all. I think staying in closer touch with nature will help me on my Journey. I need to get out of the house and off of the computer.

3. You study all you can about your Journey, and on the day of the imaginary test for this imaginary class, Professor [your response from number three, a noncorporeal being] comes in and you wonder, how will I get a good grade on your Journey Test from [same noncorporeal being]?

Gwen C. wrote for response number three:

I started crying when I did this, but now I'm smiling and so happy. My grandmother was a very quiet woman and I think sometimes put up with a lot from my grandfather, but when I asked her what I should do to get a good grade from her on this, she said I was thinking too small and I needed to stop being afraid of what other people think of me and what I'm doing. There's nothing to ever be afraid of.

How was the exercise for you? Now that you have identified three new possible mentors, let's stay out of the box with our thinking.

What animals have mentored you in your life? What animal symbol guides you? What do you see in that animal that teaches you how to behave or move forward on this part of your

Journey?

What natural elements do you gravitate to? Is there a natural element that represents attributes (skills) you need for your Hero's Journey?

What noncorporeal entities are mentors for you? Whether they were human at one time or not, whether others believe in them or not, what do *you* believe? How do they assist you?

If you let go of your limiting ideas of a mentor, the whole world will help you on your Journey.

Along with guidance, a mentor may give you a gift to use on your Journey, and the gift may have magical powers. In *The Golden Compass,* The Master gives Lyra an alethiometer that "tells you the truth." Dumbledore gave Harry the Cloak of Invisibility in *Harry Potter and the Sorcerer's Stone,* enabling him to move around unseen. Dorothy received the ruby slippers from Glenda, the Witch of the North, during her trip in Oz. In Mozart's *The Magic Flute,* the Hero Talimo is given the eponymous magic flute and magic bells, to help him rescue the Princess Pamina.

Open your eyes! What powerful, magical gifts have you been given?

What do you need to do today to keep moving on your Hero's Journey?

Get at least one mentor on board for your team.

Inventory your Mentors and Allies. What are their strengths? What skills will they bring to help you? What kind of mentor do you need right now? If you don't have one that's perfect for this stage, how could you find one? Start asking! Start by asking your allies for help finding the right mentor for where you are. At another stage, you may need a different mentor.

That's okay.

Many people will help you for free *just because you asked.* Let them give you this gift.

Chapter 6. One Step Across the Threshold

"Step into the fire of self-discovery. This fire will not burn you, it will only burn what you are not."—Mooji

What's This Hero's Journey Stage About?

You did it! You took that first step onto the Journey, you brave soul! You've stepped across a big ole' ditch, and somehow, maybe you're not even sure how, this world is different from the one you left when you took that one step. You're going to run into Guardians right away who will test your commitment, but you've got this!

Once you cross the threshold into your Hero's Journey, you are in a new world. Take a moment to acknowledge and feel what this feels like. It's a different world, and you are different—just from the one decision you made a moment ago to take that first step and answer your Call. You have joined your sisters on a Journey. Welcome!

What makes this new world different? You do. The world is now filtered through your Journey eyes. When you are different, you see the world differently. There are dragons to slay, wonders to behold, and magic to seize. Your new world is populated by strange creatures and fantastic people.

How different did the world look to Dorothy once she stepped out of her tornado-tumbled farmhouse into the land of Oz? How about Alice? Once she fell through the looking glass, Alice left the house and walked toward a beautiful garden in the distance, but every time she tried to follow the path to the garden she found herself back at the door to the house. Meg, in a *Wrinkle in Time*, is in the total darkness of "nothingness" when she "wrinkles" into a new dimension where she meets Mrs. Who, Mrs. Which, and Mrs. Whatsit. This is not the Ordinary World!

Think how a visit back to a place you visited as a child looks completely different—and not just in size—when you return as an adult. The monster in the dank cellar is just a loud clanking furnace. The creaky attic triggers nostalgia for your toys and grandfather's old army uniform. The backyard trees tower over you now. You see that the crabby neighbor is just lonely. You wonder how an entire neighborhood of kids could have fit into one yard to play red rover on a summer evening

The biggest difference in this new world is that you know there is an Adventure awaiting you.

Once I decided to be honest about my Journeys, even when the information fit naturally into the situation or conversation, I was uncomfortable telling people about my Journeys. I belong to a wonderful writers' group where I live, near Madison, Wisconsin. When I came up for rotation to submit a piece, I balked. They were used to me submitting poetry. You never really have to explain poetry! Now I had to come out to whole group of people and share my personal and spiritual beliefs. Worse than criticism, I feared the "meh . . ." response or the "Who will want to read *this*?" response.

When I took that step across the threshold from my old world and into the new, I was met quickly by Guardians of that gate. Insecurity and fear snarled at me like a junkyard dog.

The Guardian is not in the real world. It lives in the new, fantastic world—the one you've just stepped into. It never reaches over the threshold and pulls you in. You can't even see it from where you were. Once you take that first the step into the new world, bam! There it is. Cerberus, St. Peter, Inigo Montoya, and Monty Python's bridge-keeper are all examples of Guardians of the Threshold.

Guardians are there to remind you of the sanctity of the place you are entering. You just have to remember that you are worthy of passing.

Many of our significant buildings have visible, intimidating Guardians. The New York Public Library entrance is flanked by two huge lion Guardians. Temple doors are guarded by dragons. Notre Dame has gargoyles perched on the corners of the roof. These statues remind us of the power located within. Are you strong enough to pass through?

Years ago, when I visited Thailand, the family I stayed with took me to tour the Grand Palace in Bangkok. Sixteen-foot tall, bejeweled, ceramic demon-guards flank the doors. The morning after our tour, I recounted a disturbing dream I'd had that night. The statue guards we had seen the day before were walking around in my dream. The Thai family all nodded. My dream wasn't at all odd to them. They told me that's what the guards do. They walk around at night. That's how they protect the palace.

Prepare to Meet a Guardian

It is a conundrum: You have to be prepared to meet a Guardian once you cross the threshold into the new world, but you have no idea how it will show up. You can't see it from your old point of view. You must cross the threshold to encounter it. It might just be one thing, or it might be an entire brigade.

You are in a new world now. How can you prepare to meet a Guardian?

Pull up Your Socks

Know that a Guardian is there. If you haven't seen one yet, it's coming. The first way you can prepare for the Guardian is by remembering that, just like you, it has a job to do.

Guardians protect the path into the new world, the world of Adventure, the world where you will learn the magic. The Guardian's job is to question your willingness, sincerity, and commitment to undergo your Hero's Journey. Your job is to remember you have whatever it takes to meet their challenge.

Sylvia B. became a consulting Patient Advocate to help others navigate the morass of health insurance when they find out a new and frightening diagnosis. She found that short books of FAQs (Frequently Asked Questions) are the easiest for patients to use, since their ability to think clearly and to deal with insurance and government language are compromised when most of their attention is on their health. The day after she sent her FAQs book to the printer, the government made legislative changes that required changes to the answers she had provided in the book. Sylvia worked most of the night to turn around copy quickly enough to meet the publisher's deadline. A few weeks later, just after the books were printed, the government made another change, so Sylvia hustled again to prepare a slip-in page for her book.

To this date Sylvia has made over thirty changes to her book to keep up with the government's changes. She knows she could do all of her instructions online and be able to respond more quickly to regulatory changes, but she believes it helps the people she works with to have something tangible to hold in their hands for answers. She says she will keep her commitment to her patient-clients no matter what the government throws in her path.

Adjust Your Glasses

Know that the Guardian can be a shape-shifter. What looks at first like a foe might turn into a powerful ally or a mentor. In *The Princess Bride*, Inigo Montoya admires Westley, even as he fights him when they meet on the cliff top. By the end of the story, Inigo has become Westley's ally in rescuing Buttercup from the sleazy Prince Humperdink.

53

Shape-shifters are quite common on your Journey. Do you have friends or family who question your Journey? Do you have a friend or a family member who seems antagonistic but also has good advice for you? Always remember the Guardian's job! When you have to deal with Guardians, use them to remind yourself that you are committed to your Hero's Journey.

When you encounter a shape-shifter, you may be inclined to run in the other direction. Now is not the time to shut those people out of your life. Now is the time to use special gifts to get past the Guardian.

Use Your Gifts

You must use your gifts to get past the Guardian at the Threshold. You know now that the Guardian has a critical job to do on your Hero's Journey. A Guardian can be dispatched only by using your gifts—the gifts unique to you.

What are your gifts? Can you make people laugh? Are you an artist? Are you doggedly persistent? The Guardian at the Threshold is a Guardian particularly for *your* Hero's Journey. It will succumb to a weapon made of only your gifts.

Sherry H., whose Journey called her to build a school in Ethiopia, ran smack into a Guardian right after she returned from Africa: The project she was working on as consultant was cancelled. When this job loss happened, Sherry still thought she had to provide all the money for building the school herself. After some soul searching and praying, she realized she could use her skills as a project manager to break down the tasks she knew about into very small, very cheap steps. This way she knew she could keep moving, albeit slowly, but not lose her commitment to build the school.

THE ASKELLADEN ("ASH LAD")

In these traditional Norwegian tales, the Ash Lad

is always the unexpected hero. He is the tiny
(sometimes described as "deformed") boy who
sleeps on the hearth to keep the fire going
throughout the night. He doesn't have size or
might, but he still comes out on top. In one story,
he outmaneuvers a troll by his wits and clever
trickery. He bets a giant troll that if can eat more
than the troll can, the troll must let him go. The
Ash Lad pretends to slit his belly (it's really a
knapsack) to add more food. When he
challenges the troll to do the same, guess who
wins?

Understanding archetypes can help you recognize and
work with people you encounter on your Hero's Journey. An
archetype is defined as a very typical (maybe even ideal)
example of a certain person or thing, or a recurrent symbol or
motif in literature, art, or mythology. The concept of archetypes
goes back to Plato, who thought they were mental forms that
were imprinted in the soul. The psychiatrist and founder of
analytic psychology Carl Jung wrote that archetypes were innate,
universal prototypes for ideas and may be used to interpret
observations, as in dreams, stories (myths), or the repeating life
patterns of all people and all cultures. Sounds like the concept of
the monomyth, doesn't it?

The first archetype on your Journey is the Hero. You
know plenty of examples of her, and of course you are the Hero
of this Journey. You also have at least one other personal
archetype. What I call a personal archetype is a distillation of the
essential, useful attributes that make you distinct—make you,
you. This personal archetype is a symbol of your unique
combination of skills. I like to think of it as an action figure of

you that reminds you of your strongest attributes and the ones most useful to you on your Journey in addition to the Hero. Your personal archetype and its particular assets are what you must use to get past the threshold Guardians. Like your archetype, the Guardians you encounter will be unique to you and your Journey.

A friend of mine has a personal archetype of the Tinkerer. Another friend is the Dancer. Each personal archetype comes with unique skills and attributes that, when called upon, help the owner on her Hero's Journey. Jeff P., the Tinkerer, brings not just mechanical ability but the ability to use what's just "lying around the garage" to create something new or improve one of his other tools. He is constantly tweaking processes and machines to make them better, faster, or cheaper. For Jeff, coach of a high school robotics team with nearly no funding, this archetype comes in handy.

Jennifer W., the Dancer, hasn't let a stroke stop her from returning to daily practice and teaching weekly dance classes. She will repeat a movement thousands of times in practice to be able to demonstrate it without conscious thought and respond to her students with her full attention.

What does your personal archetype remind you to do? Your best tool is going to be developing the skills of that personal archetype to assist you as the Hero. Tapping into those skills will be your secret weapon. The powers that guard each stage's threshold are dangerous, and dealing with them is personally risky. Like all heroes, if you call on your competence and courage, the danger and your fears both fade.

There are many books available to explain archetypes, but I think the most interesting one is by the poet, Dominique Christina, *This Is Woman's Work*. She describes universal female archetypes that, if you identify as female or have a well-developed feminine aspect, you will recognize in yourself and your friends. This is another layer to your archetypes and another aspect of yourself that will assist you on the Journey. The archetype that I think is most relevant to her work is the "Journey Woman":

> She is interested in a tempest experience as
>
> much as a valley experience. Because experience
>
> is what calls to her from within. Remember, she
>
> is seeking to investigate the matter of this world.
>
> She wants to hold it in her hands, examine its
>
> geography, toss herself into the middle, see
>
> what her spine is made of.

This is *you* she's talking about! You are not afraid (well, maybe a little) to shake things up, to change your world. You like causing a stir, a tempest, as much as you like a restful day in the valley. Your Call to Adventure and curiosity drive you. You are willing to test yourself to get what you want. While the personal archetype is another layer of *you*—like your fingerprint, these feminine archetypes represent more universal aspects of your personality.

Combined together, the archetypes of the Hero, your feminine archetype, and your own personal archetype will awaken skills you must engage to complete your Hero's Journey successfully. As you go through the Journey you will come to realize that you have *always* had these skills.

Exercise: Finding your Personal Archetype

You could inventory your own gifts, but you may be blind to some of the best ones. So, you will have to ask your friends what your best skills are.

1. Pick at least three friends, ideally from different parts of your life.

2. Ask each of them to name your three greatest skills. Make a list.

Your list will overlap because your different friends will see different aspects of you, but there will be common attributes.

3. Create your own image to represent this archetype of you. What image comes to mind when you review that list of attributes? It is the ideal representation of you exhibiting those skills and attributes.

When I did this exercise with friends, all of them put patience as a skill for me. I would have never said that about myself! With some of the other skills they listed, I created an archetype for myself of the Gardener. I selected an image online to use for the picture and, with PowerPoint, created my own archetype.

My Gardener archetype shows up to remind me I *am* patient, and everything doesn't happen instantly. Even though I can't see a tree growing, I know it is. A gardener must be diligent and weed, mulch, and prune consistently to maintain a garden. A gardener must not recoil at dirt, worms, or sweat.

You're going to need your special powers now that you are moving into the Tests and Trials stage.

What do you need to do today to keep moving on your Hero's Journey?

Stop thinking about your shortcomings or what skills you don't have. Use what you're good at to overcome the Guardians you'll encounter. The skills you possess to defeat the demons are almost magical. It's as if they were created *just for you.* Hint: They were. Once you accept that, you will be able to get past most any roadblock.

Chapter 7. Tests and Trials

"Not everything that is faced can be changed.
But nothing can be changed until it is faced."—
James Baldwin

What's This Hero's Journey Stage About?

The Tests and Trials stage is the time when you keep encountering problem after problem and pain after pain. It's tough. Well, that's why it's called "Tests and Trials" and not "A Day Swinging in a Hammock at the Beach." There will be emotional Tests, spiritual Tests, and physical Tests, sometimes all in the same Test. These Tests are all necessary to make you stronger, more resilient, and more equipped to complete your Hero's Journey. This stage has no determinate length.

This is the part of the Journey that stops almost everyone, especially those who have had fate send them on a Journey. Now that you have set out deliberately on a Hero's Journey, you will have gotten to this part FAST. Deliberately choosing a Trial—often, it's a physical Trial—may be the easiest way to get yourself smack dab into the middle of the Journey. Otherwise, you're just sitting at home thinking about adventure.

Cheryl Strayed's story, *Wild*, is a clear example of someone setting out on purpose, directly into the physical Trial of her Hero's Journey. In *Wild*, Strayed recounts her solo hike of the Pacific Crest Trail—a walk from high-desert in Southern California to the Bridge of the Gods at the Washington state border.

I initiated a physical test for myself to start one of my Journeys. I started small, I admit it. Infinitesimal when compared to Strayed's hike. I wanted to sleep outside, on the ground, by myself. This test catalyzed my own Tests and Trials stage and initiated me for a shamanic vision quest to come.

I decided I would spend one night alone in a state or national park, because I wanted the place to be dedicated to nature. I went to Door County peninsula in Wisconsin, a finger of land that juts out into Lake Michigan. Compared to an ocean, the Great Lakes are small, but to one human standing there on the shore, this Great Lake looks unending.

There were very few people in the park on this autumn day. I saw less than ten other people and one dog. I sat on a bench near the shore for hours, waiting for night to fall. The sky was pretty clear, and I was hoping for auroras, but I never saw any.

Once the sun dropped away, I stood and honored the four directions, the elements around me, and my body. I took my pack and found my way to the campsite. It was cool, but not cold, and the smell of fallen autumn leaves and the woods was comforting. And I was very nearly terrified.

Although I don't watch horror movies, my mind looped through slasher scenarios, causing my heart to race. Every small sound—and there were only small sounds—caught my attention. In reality, the most dangerous animal I might come across here would have been a disoriented moose or a deer tick. But the hardness of the ground, even through the padding I camped on, was a measly discomfort compared to my raging fear.

After nearly an hour of imagined mayhem, and verging on tears, I told myself, "If you die here tonight, then you die here tonight." I realized I brought all the danger into the park with me—in my mind. I was the source of all of my pain. The next thing I was aware of was the early morning light.

Tests and Trials can range from my limited "sleep on the ground outside by myself" to sailing solo across the ocean or losing the election *again* when you ran for the local school board.

The Tests are critical to show *yourself* your mettle. Tests harden your muscles, build up your stamina, and cement your resolve. Tests and Trials make you into the Hero who is capable of grabbing the magic and returning to the village.

Emotional, physical, and spiritual pain are integral to your Hero's Journey and your greater goal. This stage can't be avoided, but knowing that it's a stage just might make it a little bit easier to get through. Whatever it is, you *can* do it.

AMONDO AND THE BAOBAB TREE

The story of *Amondo and the Baobab Tree* is based upon West African tales. Hélène Ducharme and Hamadoun Kassogué developed the story into a play The story shows us how even a small child can pass through his Tests and Trials and save his village.

In the story, the Baobab tree has fallen in love with the earth. It has its roots and it has four children. The only problem is that the sun, jealous of the Baobab's love story, refuses to go to bed. It shines relentlessly and burns the earth, which begins to crack. Even the sun's heart dries up and gets lost. All the water has disappeared from the village because of a drought caused by a sun that "refuses to go to sleep."

From this Baobab, a little boy named Amondo is born—from an egg!

61

The villagers all gather around the tiny boy who's come out of the egg. The snake says, "He has all the smells. He is a child of all the families!"

The griot says, "The Baobab calls the boy because it knows who he is—that he can find the heart of the sun."

Amondo must accomplish several tasks to save the village: He must steal the hump from the humpback witch. He must honor the bone of the great griot. And he must vanquish the sorcerer who guards the Baobab.

When Amondo meets the great sorcerer, Guardian of the Baobab, he says, "I've come to vanquish you!"

"How do you plan to do that?" the sorcerer asks.

"With this basket!" Amondo replies.

"What's in the basket?"

"You!"

"Me?"

"You're my prisoner." Amondo says.

The sorcerer laughs! "Your prisoner?!"

"Yes. Look." Amondo tilts the basket he has filled with a mirror toward the sorcerer.

"What are you going on about?" he sorcerer takes the basket and looks inside it. "Oh, what do you know? I am in the basket."

"You see! The sun is no longer your master. I am," Amondo proclaims. "You are my prisoner, and I am the master of the Baobab."

With the sorcerer trapped in his image in the basket, Amondo must now go down into the heart of the Baobab and find the heart of the sun, plunge it into the earth to find the source of the water and make the rain fall. He has courage from knowing he is not going in alone. Everyone in the village and all of his ancestors are coming with him.

After Amondo starts the rain, the rainbow appears as a symbol of uniting the sky with the earth and the water. The child, Amondo, has released the world from the terrible drought.

The stories that are myths, legends, and fairy tales should not be taken as fact or historical truth, but they *are* the truth of all human consciousness. That is why we love to hear them again and again and why we identify with them so easily. Amondo is a child in this story, which reflects our own innocence and naiveté when we begin our Journey, but he is able to master the tasks set out for him with the assistance and skills that come from being a child of the entire village. Trapping the evil sorcerer in the basket by using a mirror is a clever metaphor for dropping our own ego and how we can use the reflections of others to show us ourselves. Like the Baobab's Guardian sorcerer, I bristle most at those who reflect attributes most like the ones I dislike in myself.

The monsters and demons in this stage of the Journey are projections of our shadow selves and our internal conflicts. I think that half of us shadow our weaknesses and the other half shadow our strengths. Figuring out which one you are is the challenge.

These archetypal symbols have persisted through time to show up in our stories and our dreams to remind us of our part in the collective humanity and teach us how to face and overcome these demons. As we overcome them, we move on through the Hero's Journey.

KARANA ON THE ISLAND OF THE BLUE DOLPHINS

Karana was stranded alone on an island after her people left on a ship when white men came to the island. To survive, she created a shelter from whale bone and repaired a canoe. She feared making hunting tools and weapons for she had been taught the tradition that women must not touch or use such tools "Would the weapons break in my hands at the moment when my life was in danger, which is what my father had said?" Still, she made up her mind that "no matter what befell me I would make the weapons." She tamed the alpha male of a feral dog pack, wild birds, and an injured otter, creating friends to ease her loneliness. She survived a tidal wave and a massive earthquake that destroyed most of her food stores and the tools she had built over the years.

This story is based on the true story of Juana Maria, who lived alone for 18 years on San Nicolas Island in the California Channel Islands from about 1835 to 1853. Juana Maria's story is one of raw survival. Don't give in to the urge to compare the scale of your Journey with another's Journey. Everyone's Journey is different and right-sized for them, at that time. Remember that all Hero's Journeys are cyclical, layered, and fractal. The one in which you're feeling small may show itself to be part of a much larger Journey, or it may not. The scale and pattern of your Journey become obvious only from a long view.

Reframe the Problem

Once you took the step out onto your Hero's Journey, you moved into a new world. This new world differs from the old, regular world in many ways. One way you can acknowledge this new world is to reframe your "life sucks" attitude by telling yourself that you are in the Tests and Trials stage.

Reframing means that you look at these obstacles to your goal—from troublesome to downright traumatic—and you let them trigger you into a creative solution. Say to yourself, "I am on a Hero's Journey! I am part of an epic!" So, use that time at the auto repair shop as a task-completing opportunity. You sprained your ankle? Use your crutch to swipe the path clear in front of you. You're stuck on hold with your medical insurance company? Compose a song to their hold music to convey your message. Sing it to the customer service representative who

65

finally answers. After all, "This call is being recorded for customer service and training opportunities." I guarantee everyone in that department will hear your message.

I know it sounds easy and can be hard to do. How can you reframe your obstacles?

Ask for Help

I say that a lot, don't I?

Some mentors are there to guide you just through the physical Tests; they will instruct you how to get through this stage. Tests will be emotional and spiritual as well as physical. Other mentors are there to guide you through the emotional toll the Journey's Tests will take on you. More than one mentor here can be beneficial, as they will afford you more help, and each mentor can excel in her special skill area. Allies and mentors can help you see your situation from a different point of view.

Trust Another Person

Trust is critical. During the Journey, you may feel threatened and afraid, but if you do not share your fears with someone you can count on, it's not a Hero's Journey. Even if those fears seem small or petty to you, a big lesson you will need to learn on the Hero's Journey is to show your vulnerability and still be accepted. Once you open your armor, that openness allows you to *receive* help. You will never *really* learn anything until you first learn to ask for help from someone else. That first ask will be the hardest.

When you are in a twelve-step program, you have your sponsor, but you also have every other member of that group (allies) to provide you trusted guidance. Sometimes, the only thing those allies can bring you is their "two steps ahead of you on the path" experience. Look around you, reach out on social media. When you are brave enough to ask for assistance, you will always receive it. Ask. People will relish helping you.

A Pilgrimage

A pilgrimage is one long Trial, with several Subtests thrown in for good measure. The world's major religions have sacred sites, and the faithful make once-in-a-lifetime trips to experience them and confirm their faith: Mecca in Islam, Jerusalem in Judaism, Camino de Santiago in Christianity, Mt. Kailas in Bön, Buddhism, Hinduism and Jainism.

THE HUICHOL'S PILGRIMAGE FOR PEYOTE

The Huichol maize (corn) farmers of northern Mexico go on a pilgrimage for peyote, because "in Huichol religious thought, deer, maize, and peyote fit together: Maize cannot grow without deer blood; the deer cannot be sacrificed until after the peyote hunt; the ceremony that brings the rain cannot be held without peyote; and the peyote cannot be hunted until maize has been cleaned and sanctified."

A pilgrimage must be first undertaken to find the peyote, beginning an approximate 350-mile trek. To the Huichol, peyote is Wirikuta, "the original homeland," where the First People, both deities and ancestors, once lived. After they have "captured" the peyote plant by shooting two arrows into it, a shaman places peyote in each pilgrim's mouth and the group then begins to gather peyote for the rest of the community.

To the Huichol people, peyote is not a
recreational drug (as you may think of it). It is
integral to their lives and a necessary ritual for
their community's spiritual well-being. While on
your Journey, you may do things that others see
as frivolous or even bizarre, but you know those
acts are important to you personally and to your
Journey. Keep on it!

Your Hero's Journey may have a pilgrimage with mostly
an emotional impact. An adult who was adopted may search for
her roots by looking for her biological parents. This part of the
Journey will have administrative and logistical Trials, but be
dominated by the emotional Trial.

Sherry H.'s Journey to build a school in Ethiopia has
been supported by her children's support and faith in her goal.
Her biggest Test so far was the idea that she had to provide all
the money and do all the work herself. When she told me about
her goal, I said that I would like to help her, and I wanted to give
her money just so I could see her do this thing she wanted to do.

Sherry hired a coach to keep her on track, asked other
school-builders how they did it, and created a fund-raising page.
Sherry's discovering how to rely on the benign power that she
believes called her to this Journey and supports her during this
rough passage.

It is possible your Journey's Tests and Trial will be one
occurrence, although that is highly unlikely. It's more likely the
Tests will take place over a long period and repeat themselves.
Janet's Hero's Journey for yoga certification took six months
and a commitment to follow the training schedule, giving up all
of her summer holidays and weekends to attend classes.

The worst part of the Tests and Trials stage for me is that I feel like I'm not in control of what's happening. I get frustrated, angry, and hurt. Maybe this is what you experience at this stage, too. You know these Trials are blocking you from reaching your goal, but you don't know what to do to get past them. Let's come up with a way to get through (or around, under, or over) the obstacles.

Exercise: What Would the Movie Hero Do Now?

Look at your current obstacle to your goal (a Test or Trial). Whether you are having car trouble, teenager trouble, or health trouble, you can use this exercise to reframe your situation and shift your point of view. In reframing the problem, you are likely to come up with a helper, a solution, or both.

Imagine you are the director of a movie that tells the story of your Hero's Journey. Imagine how you want this scene to play out. A caution—you don't want this scene to win you an Academy Award for emotional range. You want the story to move on, ideally to the next stage of your Journey.

1. You are the hero of your movie. Describe the problem (what is happening to you) as if it is happening on a movie screen. Cast an actor in to play the part of you.

2. How would you, as the movie hero, react to the problem?

3. Your movie hero knows what she wants to get done here. If you are she, with your own problem right now, what do you want to happen?

4. Movie heroes usually learn a lesson from their problems? What lesson could you be learning right

now from your current problem?

5. How does this problem or situation move you, the movie hero, closer to your goal?

Have you ever helped a baby learn to walk? For those of you without children of your own, have you seen a baby learn to walk? Okay. When the baby takes her first few wobbles and drops to her butt, does anyone in the room say, "Forget it! You blew it! That was terrible! Don't even bother to try that again."?

Of course you wouldn't do that. So why aren't you as forgiving to yourself in your own wobbles?

The Brady Bill, which made background checks a requirement for gun purchases from licensed dealers, took twelve years to get signed from the day James Brady and President Ronald Regan were shot.

Mothers Against Drunk Driving (MADD) took six years to get the concept of "designated driver" into the public mindset.

Megan's law, to require authorities to notify communities of the whereabouts of convicted sex offenders, took over two years to enact—even with the impetus of the death of a child.

You must first be brave enough to acknowledge your weaknesses and shadows to stare down those demons when they pop up over and over again on your Journey. Working through your Tests and Trials builds your stamina to keep going from this stage forward. Jung said this effort is essential for any self-knowledge. You are earning the coming reward by going through this stage.

What do you need to do today to keep moving on your Hero's Journey?

Get help on just one problem you're facing. Sometimes just talking about the problem with an ally or mentor kicks a solution into gear, but even more useful is to ask your mentor or ally for assistance.

Acknowledge how you feel during this stage. You may feel like you will be stuck in this swamp of a stage forever, but you won't be. You just have to keep telling yourself, "It's a stage. It has an end. It's a stage. It has an end."

Chapter 8. Change Your Approach

"When we are no longer able to change a situation—we are challenged to change ourselves."—Viktor E. Frankl

What's This Hero's Journey Stage About?

This stage is where you feel close to your goal. And you probably are. You may be able to see it from where you are. But you may also be bogged down in some sticky Tests and Trials and need a way out. A good way out is to change your approach by shifting things around and shaking things up. A fresh approach will get you un-stuck and into the next stage.

It's closer. You can feel it. It's there on the horizon. Maybe you can even see it if you stretch out some.

I felt the Call to share my shamanic gifts with others. I had taken classes, worked with teachers and a coach, and read (a lot) on the subject. What I hadn't been brave enough to do was actually "do it" with another person. One hot July night last year, although the air conditioning was on, I was having trouble falling asleep, so I started a visioning meditation. My knees hurt from a long walk I had taken that morning, so I rubbed my heel onto a tender spot on the inward side of my leg. A vision came without any ramp-up: I am running from the warrior. He reaches toward me and his war club cleaves my head. I slip down, first to my knees and then completely flat. I watch my sisters keep running into the dark. I think, "At least my sisters have gotten away." Then I am looking at my body on the ground from across a lake with a nearly full moon reflected off its surface. I see this experience as showing my connection to all women through our pain.

The comedian Amy Poehler said, "The doing is the

thing. The talking and worrying and thinking are not the thing." I finally had the courage to step out. I had to sit down next to a live human, hold her hand, and let the first shared vision happen. Oh, jeepers, was I frightened—mostly of how I could fail—until it started, then the universe took over for me, and we both had a wonder-filled, shared experience.

If you have reached the Approach stage, you are climbing down and into the deepest part of your Journey. This is the point where you will differentiate between the illusion—all of that crap in your head—and truth. Things you thought were true about yourself are now being shown to you to be the greatest illusions you have ever seen. Houdini has nothing on you. The greatest Ordeal is just around the corner, so this is a good place for a **Rest Stop** (just a bit) so you are prepared for the next stage. Olden days' Heroes would be seen resting by the fire, cleaning their weapons, knowing a great battle will take place the next day. For you, it's a metaphoric next day.

On the Hero's Journey, the Approach is about being closer to your goal and how you get to the goal. On a Hero's Journey, you have to change how you do things as much you have to do "the thing."

At this point, you are may be exhausted from enduring the Tests. Through the pain of the Tests and Trials you keep bumping up against the edge of your goal. Maybe you feel like you're doing that "one step forward, two steps back" dance. Maybe you put your Hero's Journey on the shelf for a while. Maybe it was a long while. It doesn't matter. The Hero's Journey has no prescribed duration. Odysseus sailed around for ten years before making it home after the Trojan War. He got his own epic poem. You deserve one, too.

Changing your approach is the best way to pull yourself out of the Tests and Trials stage of the Hero's Journey and get to your reward—to seize the magic.

How do you change your approach? Like they say in the twelve-step programs, it's not easy, but it's simple.

Call on a Mentor

You don't ask for help a lot, do you? I know I don't. This is the first change of approach change you need to make. Start with a mentor you used in previous stages. Can she help you flip your approach around?

Think about getting a mentor just for this stage. How about crowd-sourcing a mentor? How about bartering your time with someone to mentor each other?

How do you get yourself to ask for help? I had to stop thinking that asking for help was all about me. It's not. Since I believe we are all connected, when you engage a mentor you are catalyzing a new part of *her* Journey. Your role on someone else's Journey is proof of the fractal nature of all Hero's Journey stories. You don't need to see their Journey; you just need to know that asking for help is letting someone experience the joy of giving. It is facilitating another person's Hero's Journey. Let's remember that.

Reframe

Some Trials we bring on ourselves just because we have an idea of what the magic or the message should be like. We get stuck in our point of view. How do you think what you're doing will be viewed by others? Other points of view are what Mentors and Allies excel at. Like the fish who asks, "Water? What's water?" you can't see what you're inside of. You need someone else to show you from an outside perspective.

A HUNTER WHEN THE WORLD BEGAN

In this story, the hunter's normal hunting tools and methods would not work against a monstrous creature. He had to use the unusual tools given him by an ally, the old woman he meets on his Journey.

In the Nigerian story, A Hunter When the World Began, the King of all Hunters decided to test the strength and cleverness of his son.

"I have killed all the wildest, most savage animals," he said to his son, "except one. Go out into the bush. If you are able to kill this one remaining savage creature, you will have my permission to marry.

"Remember," his father warned him, "what you are going to hunt is the most fearful animal in the world; with many mouths; with fire-like eyes; with enormous strength."

The young man took some food, then took his gun and his knife, called for his three dogs, and went off into the bush. He walked all day, and in the evening caught a hare for his supper. He walked all the next day and the day after that.

At last he came to the hut of an old woman who lived alone. She was outside her hut by a stream, where she was washing cooking-pots. She called out to him.

"I cannot stop," the young man replied, "for my business is urgent."

The old woman called to him again that it was very important for him to speak with her. The young man turned and went to see what she wanted.

"Here is food," said the old woman.

It was good food and the young man enjoyed eating it.

"Here is a calabash," said the old woman, "please wash it."

The young man went to the stream and started to wash the calabash. But as he washed it, it broke. Inside he found an egg, a round smooth stone, and a small broom of palm-raffia.

"You have broken the calabash and I am glad," said the old woman. "Take with you what you have found inside. In case of danger drop one at a time, first the egg, then the small broom, then the round smooth stone."

The young man thanked her and went on his way.

The next day the young man reached a dark

forest. He entered the forest, and at once his dogs started to bark. To his surprise, the young man suddenly saw the fearful creature which he had set out to hunt. The creature had many mouths, and fire-like eyes, and enormous strength.

The young man aimed his gun and fired, but the fearful creature only looked at him and grew bigger and bigger.

The young man made a sign to his dogs to attack the fearful creature, but having looked into the fire-like eyes, their own eyes were blinded. The young man took his knife and ran to attack the fearful creature. They fought all that day, all that night, and all the next day, but at last the young man was victorious and killed the fearful creature.

The young man was glad, for he was now certain to marry a young girl in his town, and he had destroyed a more fearful creature than any other hunter had done. The young man put the fearful creature on his back and started on his homeward Journey. He left the forest and was walking through some woods when it became dark. He lay down to sleep.

The next morning was bright and clear, but as the young man woke up, he saw coming towards him the creature come back to life and far larger than the fearful creature he had killed, far fiercer, and with far more fiery eyes.

The young man jumped up and started to run, with the wild animal following him. He remembered what the old woman had given him, and he dropped the egg. At once, there was a wide lake behind him, the greatest lake in the world. The lake slowed the animal, but it still followed him.

The hunter dropped the broom that came out of the calabash, and at once there was the largest forest in the world behind him. The animal was slowed by the trees, but still followed him. Now the young man was nearing his father's house.

Finally, he dropped the round smooth stone, and at once there stood the highest mountain in the world. At last the young man was able to reach his father's house and safety.

This is a wonderful story that can teach us many lessons. Here are some that I see: The first is to accept the gifts that our allies give us and listen to their advice. Sometimes, the tools we bring with us, like the young warrior's dogs and gun, don't help. The magic of the Hero's Journey is that we learn and pick up tools along the way. Release your expectations. You, too, could break open a gourd and find a great forest. Maybe you will find an egg that, when dropped, will create a great lake. Maybe you will remember that, though your actions are small, they still have an effect on the world. Or perhaps the monster might have been in the warrior's mind the whole time!

The Beaver and the Porcupine, a Tlingit Myth

The spiny Porcupine tribe had a grievance against the Beaver, who he had left their brother Porcupine stranded on the Beaver's lodge, plotted to take his life in revenge. The Porcupine tribe carried the Beaver to the top of a tall tree, thinking that, as the Beavers could not climb, he would be in the same plight as their brother Porcupine when left on the Beaver's island home. But by the simple expedient of eating the tree downward from the top, Beaver chewed his way home.

How can you solve your own problem by "eating the tree from the top down?" Are you brave enough to pick the problem you know is really your big blocker?

Exercise: Turn It Upside Down and Backwards

If you are finding yourself hollering up from the bottom of a deep hole, let's look at the problem differently and try a different approach to get un-stuck. How can you "wackify" your approach? The more unusual, the greater the difference from "the way you've always done it," the more likely your success, the more likely you will break your pattern.

Here are some examples:

Problem: No one was answering Marcie P.'s letters to get an environmental clean-up in her town.

Current Approach: Marcie wrote all of her letters to government officials in the evening when she felt she could concentrate and write thoughtful, cogent letters.

Upside down and Backwards: She decided to flip that around by sending a social media message (Facebook, Twitter, etc.) to the same government agencies each morning while she was eating breakfast. The messages didn't have all the detail of her letters, but were more passionate. Now that her messages were public and repeatable, she started getting responses.

Problem: Arjun wanted very much to add exercise to his daily routine, but kept finding he didn't go to the gym before or after work.

Current Approach: Arjun carried his gym bag, but more and more found he left it the car and never went to the gym.

Upside down and Backwards: He had read that shorter workouts were just as effective as long ones, and he was fortunate that the company he worked for had a small gym. He spoke with his manager and asked if he could take two half hour breaks during the work day to walk to the company gym and do some weight lifting. She agreed, and he found free half hours at varied times during the day. Because he was exercising for much shorter periods of time, but more frequently, he was never bored and kept to his new exercise routine.

All of us can get trapped by our patterns of doing things the same way, while expecting different results. If you want to break out of this stage, look for a way to change even just one part of your routine. Changing one small thing can domino change throughout your process, shake loose a logjam, and move you from this stage to the next one.

What do you need to do today to keep moving on your Hero's Journey?

Pick any one obstacle you're facing. Once you have selected the obstacle, pull in your allies and mentor (your team) and ask for their help with a new "wackified" approach to solving it. Feed and water your team while you let them work on this problem for you. With your team, you will engage the magic of synergy to create an approach that will knock this obstacle out of your way and push you further on your Journey.

Chapter 9. The Ordeal and a Death

"Once you choose hope, anything is possible."—Christopher Reeve

What's This Hero's Journey Stage About?

The Ordeal stage is a paradox. It is both the pinnacle and nadir of your Hero's Journey. You are now one hundred and eighty degrees from where you left the regular world and began. This puts you at the pinnacle. This stage is the gut-busting demise of your old self, which makes it the nadir from a personal aspect. From here, you can look straight back across the circle that is your Journey and see how far you have traveled. From here, you can look just up the hill and see the magic you've been searching for. But this stage won't be a **Rest Stop**; it will be the Ordeal.

This is the part of your story, as you speak to those gathered with you around the flickering fire, when you say, "and that's when I . . ."

A terrible Ordeal and a death! This is something to look forward to, eh? Maybe your Journey was already at this stage when you dropped into this book. Maybe you didn't even know you were on a Hero's Journey, and you're just seeing your experience in this new light for the first time.

It's hard to face going in, but something will die as a part of your Hero's Journey. Someone or something dies on *everyone's* Journey.

You are not going to welcome this Ordeal. The monster will be ferocious. It's going to hurt like a son-of-a-gun. The stuff you've been hiding from yourself and lying to yourself about will all come out. But--and it's a big but--the Ordeal will change your life and propel you through the rest of the Journey. You have to go through it; there is no shortcut. Knowing ahead of time that the stage is pivotal and it has an end can help (a little).

The grief that comes with the Ordeal may be like a hole you have fallen into and don't want to climb out of. The way a great loss often makes me just want to climb in bed, pull the covers up over my head and never come out again. That's what makes this stage of the Journey so difficult. Your pain and grief will be blinders that keep you from seeing that *you can* get out of this deep, rocky pit and get back up and finish the Journey.

The paradox is that while you cannot go on a Hero's Journey alone, the Ordeal you must face is solitary. If you thought your Tests and Trials were tough, watch out.

It feels ironic to me now, but one reason I was able to step out on my own as a shaman was that one my mentors was diagnosed with pancreatic cancer. Marshall had significant parts of his body removed, choosing to do conventional medical treatment along with shamanic and more ancient, esoteric practices.

Our conversations, practices, and rituals had always been deep, but now the stark reality of Marshall's end date colored every meeting. It seemed there was no magical cure or miracle that would show up, although we both professed to believe strongly that one was possible. I felt lame and impotent that I could not fix this for him, for I am not a healer (I am a guide). I felt resentful and angry that he was abandoning me. I was embarrassed by these feelings.

This deep and dangerous hole has been called "the belly of the whale" and "the innermost cave" by author Joseph Campbell. In it, you will be set upon by external fiends and internal demons. The external obstacles have the advantage of being visible. The internal obstacles often seem visible only to our friends, allies, and mentors.

83

For me, the internal identities are the hardest to beat because you think of them as a part of yourself, and eliminating them doesn't quite compute. How will I rid myself of what is a part of me?

Rod T. wanted to retire from his position as a professionally certified aircraft inspector. Rod had been working since he was ten years old, and even the thought of not going somewhere to work each day was nearly overwhelming. Could he abandon the letters after his name? Could he stop constantly learning new regulations, new engines, and new structures? Would he still have value if he stopped working?

Remember Luke Skywalker's disbelief when Darth Vader told him, "I am your father . . ."? Remember the look on Leia's face when Luke told her that Darth Vader was her father, too? Deep inside both characters was the great fear that they held the potential for the same evil.

In classic Greek myth, this stage meant the death of the parent or overcoming the parent and moving into adulthood. In an on-purpose Hero's Journey, you may actually experience the death of a parent or loved one, but more likely this stage is indicated by your abdicating someone else's expectation of you—their idea of who and what you should be, an identity you absorbed without even knowing you were doing it. You know that it no longer fits you or serves you, even if you don't know what or who you will be without it.

For Terri G., years of personal work to overcome an abusive relationship culminated when she had to stand her ground with her mother during a vacation in Hawaii, "She started blasting me for checking in with Tim, my autistic son, and with my work while she thought I should be resting. I decided right then I wasn't going to give up my power to *anyone*, anymore. I told her to stop, and I would decide how to spend my time." Terri said it took a few days for her and her mother to start speaking again, but when she did, it was with more respect, as two adult friends. "The funny thing was, I didn't feel the need to check in so much with work or Tim for the rest of my vacation."

Paula R's daughter had stopped eating. The teenager had been adept at hiding her goal of eating only 200 calories a day and covering her rapidly shrinking body. When Paula discovered her daughter had not been eating normally, she did what most mothers would do—she tried everything she could think of to get her daughter to eat, but the mental illness of an eating disorder exerts a terrible and tight hold on its target. When her daughter dropped to a dangerously low weight, Paula decided to take complete control of her daughter's life in order to save it. She hospitalized her and, when she was released, took over 24/7 care and monitoring. Paula abandoned all of her own adult freedoms in that moment.

As she expected, her daughter fought being told what she could and could no longer do. She rebelled at being watched nearly every moment, with all of her meals and her body tracked and recorded for months until she returned to a normal weight. Paula cries when she says this. "I had to love her enough to endure her hating me to get her well, and she did hate me then."

Completing the Ordeal requires you to make a willing sacrifice. Your choice in this stage is the culmination of your Journey into the magical world. You are saying to yourself and to those around you—who may ridicule or ostracize you—that you are doing this. You are willing to change. You are willing to give up a lot: friends, social standing, whatever. It would not be a Hero's Journey if everybody thought what you were doing was a great idea.

ALL THE HEALERS FROM FOREVER

On my visioning meditation this night, I am

cartwheeling through the sky, feet over head

85

and over again, and then wheeling between rows of trees in an orange grove. I land hard on sand on my hands and knees, then I spin up with the sand, creating a whirlwind of a sand devil. It whirls with me and around me.

I can see the grains of sand and feel them whirling through me and out through my chest. I stop turning and step outside of the whirling sand. Then I step back into it, feeling it pull me back in. I feel the grit of the sand and a sharpness, a pain in my chest. A shaman appears holding a drum hammer and hits me on my back, behind the spot where the sand comes through my chest.

I cry, "No, don't beat it out of me," arching away from him. I walk up a hill to a pool and step into the water. Many women walk up to the edge of the pool and surround me. All the healers from forever. I lean back into the embrace of one. Her large brown arms hold me and pour water over me. All the women stand on the side of the pool, then reach out and put their hands on my chest. Stacked hands forever. I curl my knees up onto my chest.

I feel an overwhelming need to massage a pain on the right side of my chest. I do and cry out, and the pain shoots out of me.

In its place was a hole; a hole filled with the pool I was in. Warm feathers dried and caressed me, and I begged for the women to help me because I couldn't do it myself. They lay their hands on their chests and I felt the pool envelop me and be in me.

RAZIA JAN AND MALALA YOUSAFZAI

Razia Jan worked for four years in Deh'Subz, Afghanistan, to build a school and convince local families and girls to come and get a free education. "The day we opened the school (on) the other side of town, they threw hand grenades in a girls' school, and 100 girls were killed. Every day, you hear that somebody's thrown acid at a girl's face . . . or they poison their water" for having the audacity to go to school. Although she is an American citizen, Jan's nonprofit keeps her Afghani school open for over 300 girls. Each day, before starting classes, the school staff checks the well for poison and the rooms for bombs.

Malala Yousafzai started advocating for girls' education in her native Pakistan when she was only eleven years old. She started with a speech called, "How dare the Taliban take away my basic right to education?" As she became more outspoken and popular, the Taliban issued a death threat against her. In 2012, when she was fifteen, Malala was shot in the head while returning home from school. She survived the assassin's attack and continues to speak out for girls' access to school. Yousafzai was awarded the Nobel Prize for Peace in 2014.

When you read that, don't you think what amazing women they are? These two contemporary women, who risk their lives to educate girls, are extreme examples of the great Ordeal as a stage of the Hero's Journey. Both Jan and Malala keep working on their Journey despite continued harassment and personal danger, yet they see themselves as ordinary women who just want something very much. They want all girls to be able to go to school. When I look at their pictures, they look just like ordinary women —their persistence and fortitude don't show on their faces--yet they embody the idea that it is *ordinary* people who do the Hero's Journey. Ordinary . . . like us.

Complex Identities and Roles

Earlier in the book, I listed the usual descriptions of someone on a Hero's Journey. The short form of that list is big, white, male. Yet, I've shown you story after story of women, all ages, sizes, education, and culture who are answering their Call. Against high odds and what even they might think of as a "woman's role," they are completing their Journey.

Even more onerous than breaking traditional gender roles, many people in our cultures still bristle at homosexuality and gender misalignment. For some, parental ideas of gender and sexuality are the most challenging to get past. Some families ostracize any child who cannot repudiate a nonconforming sexuality or gender identity. There are religions that build their idea of the afterlife on family reunification in heaven. Sinners cannot join the family in heaven.

Not becoming who our parents expect us to become, or not doing what our parents want us to do is painful for everyone. The predominant message received is, "You don't love me for who I am."

Elaine M. said, "It is incredibly painful to be disowned by your parents. I'm 50 years old now, and I came out 30 years ago when I was a sophomore in college. My parents were born-again Christians. When I came out to my mom, she told me she couldn't love me. It hurt to hear my gay friends and acquaintances talk about how they reconciled with their parents when I could not. It hurt and was scary as hell to graduate from college with no job and no home to go to."

A gay religious child must overcome both his human parents and his godparent. She may have to sacrifice her family connections. For those facing this dilemma, this Ordeal is a Hero's Journey of epically painful proportions. Yet many do it, and some embark on the Journey when very young and spend their entire lives advocating for those who come after them.

How can you get through this stage? How can you keep going?

Consult the map

When you're in pain, you might not remember the cycle-form of the Hero's Journey until someone reminds you that, once you get through this Ordeal, you are over halfway done. This is the point where you are at the deepest part of yourself (Campbell's "innermost cave," that "belly of the whale"). This Ordeal is the point where you can look back and see the old you directly across the abyss from yourself. You will know it's you, but you're nearly unrecognizable because a part of you has died.

Get Help

You really can't go through this alone. Now is the time you will be grateful for the Mentors and Allies you gathered earlier. An ally will push your butt up and boost you out of the hole you're sitting in, while a mentor will dig in her heels to pull you up. Strong Mentors and Allies see what you can't. They can point out what you're missing and show you the way back into the light.

Asking for help is still a challenge for me, but I don't want to define my life by my demons, so I have to face them. I want to learn what I need to learn from my challenges, keep growing, and get all the way through my Hero's Journey. I remind myself how good it feels when I help someone; then I can give the gift of that feeling to another easily.

Watch Your Dreams

Depending on what you believe your dreams mean, your dreams are at least a window into your own unconscious. Archetypes fill up the main roles in our dreams. I find the best way for me to understand a dream is to recount it, out loud, as soon as I wake up. Dream messages can be a direct line to your intuition, which can get muffled during waking hours.

Attend to Your Grief

Sometimes on your Journey a person in your life dies for real. This loss and the stress it comes with make the Hero's Journey feel like Dante's slog through Hell. Along with the pain of the loss, you are experiencing the pain of losing the identity part of yourself that died. If your parent has died, are you anyone's child anymore,? A gift of working through your grief is the realization that something new has been born in you as a part of the process. That's something solid to hold on to.

Exercise: Your Talisman

Because there is no one sure way to get through the Ordeal, you need all the help you can get. A valuable helper throughout your Journey is a talisman. A talisman is a protective and (maybe even) a magical object. You are likely to keep it with you at all times.

What is your talisman on your Hero's Journey?

A talisman is an object, usually made of natural materials and close to its natural state, that we imbue with power. It is usually something elemental—of the earth. A talisman can be a stone or something that was living at one point—like a clover leaf or leaf from a tree at your home; something that is petrified wood; or a crystal or amber, which sometimes has an insect or plant material preserved in it.

Your talisman will be an object that will help you "see" and one that will guide you home. A talisman represents our connections—earth, fire, or water, something that represents the elements.

A talisman is a grounding mechanism; it is a reminder mechanism. It is an object that is a reminder of love.

My friend, Jana, said, "I am wondering why I haven't one. Should I have one? I haven't had a talisman for years and I have managed quite well without it, although maybe not as well as I would have done."

Like Jana, you may say you don't have a talisman, but many people have one without owning up to it. Often, they say, "Oh, no, no, I don't have one of those." But they have a keychain they've kept for twenty years or a piece of jewelry that belonged to their mother, and even if they don't wear it, they keep it with them all the time. There might be something lurking around your home or at the bottom of your purse or bag. Something you keep carrying. An object you can't let go of.

While talking about talismans, Jana remembered, "Well, I used to have a talisman of a different sort. The last one I had was maybe one or two years ago. It was a rose quartz, and it was shaped in a little heart, and it was for reminding me to take care of my own broken heart."

There is everything right with keeping something that reminds you to be your best self, that reminds you of someone you love, or to love yourself. That's all a talisman is; it is a powerful reminder. It has no power on its own. Its power comes from what it helps you believe about yourself. A talisman connects you consciously to the Journey.

The talisman will serve to remind you that every stage has an end, and the Hero's Journey itself has an end, but it will also remind you that you're part of all that is and that you must have help along the way. You carry your talisman for what you've accomplished, for where you were, and for where you are going.

Have you found your talisman? Keep it with you on this Journey.

The Ordeal stage transforms you into the person capable of grasping the magic and receiving the message to carry back to the village. You cannot get through the next stage without having built your muscles during the Trials. The Ordeal also transports you, like a giant water-slide, into the next stage of your Journey. Recognizing that you are close to the magic is critical. If you stop your Journey now, you may find yourself forever troubled by the demon, What-might-have-been. Let's buckle up and get through to the other side.

What do you need to do today to keep moving on your Hero's Journey?

Although your pain will keep you feeling inert, you must do two things:

1. Remember that this Ordeal is a part of your Hero's Journey and to make all the previous work and pain worthwhile, you have to keep moving. Reaching your goal will mitigate the pain of your Ordeal.
2. Reach out for the assistance you need so you can be equipped for the next stage.

Chapter 10. You Seize the Magic

"Knowledge is like a Baobab tree; one person's arms cannot encompass it."—Ghanaian Proverb

What's This Hero's Journey Stage About?

The stage for "Seize the Magic" is when you realize you have just met a goal (or had a big revelation or made a breakthrough) for your Journey. What may surprise you most is this is always the shortest stage.

Your Hero's Journey is as unique as you are. Truly, only *you* can achieve *this* goal. It is as unique as your fingerprint and your iris, because your touch and your vision are what make this Journey worthwhile for you and for the world. When Bill Moyers interviewed Joseph Campbell, Moyers commented, "Unlike the classical Heroes, we're not going on our Journey to save the world, but to save ourselves." To which Campbell replied, "And in doing that, you save the world."

If one were to find the Holy Grail, the grail would give the finder eternal life and spiritual understanding. When you go on a Hero's Journey on purpose, what I'm calling the "magic" is your newfound treasure of awareness, knowledge, and enlightenment. Having the magic is what you've been working toward all of this time. Once you seize the magic, you have the power of that magic in you. You will be able to use the magic.

If you have gotten to this stage already—great! This part is what you've been working toward. You've gotten to your goal: you know that you've made big changes; or you have the cure; or you've won the contest. Whatever "it" is, you've reached that goal.

If you haven't quite made it (or you are not sure if you

have), keep reading anyway. The stages of your Journey rarely have clear edges. Sometimes the only way you know you've entered a new stage is when you're near the end of it, or an ally or mentor points it out to you.

If your goal was to climb a mountain, you have made a step and realized there's no more up to step up onto. If your Call was to start a counseling practice, and you've met with your first client, you've done what you set out to do. That's why this stage of your Hero's Journey is the shortest. Seizing the magic takes just a moment. It may be a quiet moment when you realize, "Hey, I did it," just after you did it.

I had been using my skills for shamanic visioning meditation for myself for a few years. I learned many things and was always entranced by what I saw and felt. I knew I was called to share this skill with others and take them with me—to see what we could see together or what I could show them. The moment after I took a friend through a visioning meditation with me, I realized that I had just done what I had been terrified to do. The realization took only a moment. I had to put my feelings aside right then to be present with her and her feelings. Later, when I had some time for myself, I did my own **Rest Stop**. I started giggling, then really laughed, realizing that I had just reached my goal!

Beyond the realization of accomplishment, seizing the magic will give you powers and skills you didn't have before you undertook this Journey. From this point on, you can begin to use them. Wherever you are in life, you are on a Hero's Journey. If you take control of it, you can bring the magic into your life and the lives of others. Like all new skills you may flop around a little at first as you get the hang of it. As you use your new skills more and more, you become adept.

To get to this stage, you have had a lot of help along the way, but no one can hand you the magic. You must grab it yourself.

The Once and Future King

In T. H. White's Arthur story, *The Once and Future King*, Wart (who will later become King Arthur) seizes the magic while he is trying to find a sword for this brother to use. Depending on what you choose to believe, he received the magic accidentally or by Divine Providence.

In the story, Wart (Arthur) needed to find a sword for his brother, Sir Kay, to compete in the Joust. Finding their inn locked, Wart searched London and came upon what he thought was a war memorial, with a sword set in an anvil in a stone.

""People," cried the Wart, "I must take this sword. It is not for me, but for Kay. I will bring it back."

There was still no answer, and Wart turned back to the anvil. He saw the golden letters, which he did not read, and the jewels on the pommel, flashing in the lovely light.

"Come, sword," said the Wart.

He took hold of the handles with both hands and strained against the stone. There was a melodious consort on the recorders, but nothing moved.

The Wart let go of the handles, when they were beginning to bite into the palms of his hands, and stepped back, seeing stars.

"It is well fixed," he said.

He took hold of it again and pulled with all his might. The music played more strongly, and the light all about the churchyard glowed like amethysts; but the sword still stuck.

"Oh, Merlyn," cried the Wart, "help me to get this weapon."

There was a kind of rushing noise, and a long chord played along with it. All around the churchyard there were hundreds of old friends. They rose over the church wall all together, like the Punch and Judy ghosts of remembered days, and there were badgers and nightingales and vulgar crows and hares and wild geese and falcons and fishes and dogs and dainty unicorns and solitary wasps and corkindrills and hedgehogs and griffins and the thousand other animals he had met. They loomed round the church wall, the lovers and helpers of the Wart, and they all spoke solemnly in turn. Some of them had come from the banners in the church,

where they were painted in heraldry, some from
the waters and the sky and the fields about—but
all, down to the smallest shrew mouse, had
come to help on account of love. Wart felt his
power grow . . .

The Wart walked up to the great sword for the
third time. He put out his right hand softly and
drew it out as gently as from a scabbard.

Wart's life shifts dramatically from this point in the story, as will
yours once you seize the magic.

Once you do seize it, you will have earned your feelings
of accomplishment and success. You should celebrate. You've
learned great lessons by surviving the Trials and Ordeals up until
this point.

Reaching this part of your Hero's Journey doesn't mean
all your problems have gone away. It means only that you now
have answers and have reached the top of the mountain. You've
planted your flag. Take a deep breath, because now you will
have to decide what to do next.

*What do you need to do today to keep moving on your
Hero's Journey?*

For today, just take a moment to pause and reflect on all
you have accomplished and how far you have come on this
Journey. Tick off what you have gone through emotionally,
physically, and spiritually. Notice how you have changed. Take a
Rest Stop to recognize what a magnificent being you are to have
done all that you have.

Chapter 11. The Long and Winding Road Back

"The reason I finished [my first book] is that I finally came to understand that the only thing worse than having to really, truly write the whole damn thing was having to live with the fact that I didn't."—Cheryl Strayed

What's This Hero's Journey Stage About?

The stage called "the Road Back" begins the process of taking you back to the regular world and out of the fantastic world. On the Road Back you may repeat parts of the previous stages, but you will keep moving back to your village.

Here's a good place for a **Rest Stop**. Sit down and think. There's a **Rest Stop** built in here on purpose. You've grabbed the magic elixir. You're still nursing some boo-boos from the previous stages. What I am going to say next may surprise you.

It's okay to leave your Hero's Journey unfinished.

Huh?

It's okay to stop here and leave your Journey unfinished. Really. Truly.

You've learned a lot. You've overcome all kinds of demons and shone a flashlight into the dark corners of your personal shadows. Your "ah-ha" moments were many. Why would you even *think* about going back to the regular world? It's nice here reveling in your new awareness and knowledge. Keeping it all to yourself is very tempting.

You would be in good company if you decided to stop now. In the Oz book series, Dorothy eventually returns to Oz and stays with her new friends. She returns to Kansas in the first book, *The Wonderful Wizard of Oz,* and in the movie. In *Frozen*, Elsa struggled to decide whether to stay in her ice castle up in the mountains where she believed she wouldn't hurt anyone, but was far away from her family and royal subjects. Siddhartha (The Buddha) could have sat back down under the Bodhi tree after he achieved enlightenment. He wondered whether his realization could even be taught to others.

The Greek goddess of fire and home, Hestia, never left Mt. Olympus to visit earth. Some of the characters of *Lost Horizon*, a story of the fabled Shangri-La, decided to stay and live forever in their paradise rather than return to their homes. Modern examples include author J. D. Salinger, actress Greta Garbo, and publisher William Randolph Hearst, who all holed-up in their private Shangri-La. Stories abound of Catholic Saints, like St. Teresa of Avila and St. Joseph of Cupertino, who died in a state of ecstasy.

The Road Back to the Ordinary World is, I think, the most challenging part of the whole Hero's Journey. It is the least sexy, but the most personally challenging of the stages. You've conquered obstacles, integrated great changes in yourself, and grabbed the magic elixir. You answered the Call to Adventure, and you got some! Now the hard part.

The Road Back is the most difficult because first you must decide whether or not you *want* to go back to the Ordinary World *and* whether or not you want to bring the magic back to your village and share it with others.

ODYSSEUS

In *The Odyssey*, Odysseus battled Polyphemus, Scylla, Charybdis, Sirens, and more. He delved into the underworld, where he nearly died. He had adventures, yes, but he also left behind his wife and family over ten years earlier. He is tired now and has some regret for his diversions and dallying. Finally, as we saw earlier, at the court of the king and queen of Phaeacia, he recounts his travels and Trials and begs for assistance to return home—where he's been trying to get for ten years.

If you decide to move on, you have to remember how messy the real world is, how banal. You must remember what it was like when you were not the Hero of the story. Remember all of what returning to the real world will be like, and decide if you want to do it anyway.

So why return?

HARRIET TUBMAN

Harriet Tubman traveled the ultimate Road Back after her own Journey to freedom. She went back into slave territory innumerable times to lead others to freedom. She kept no diary, nor is there any record describing her decision to return—she was illiterate. It's known only that shortly after reaching freedom in Philadelphia she decided to risk returning to the South to bring more slaves to freedom. In an interview forty years later, Tubman said, "I felt like Moses. De Lord tole me to do dis. I said, 'Oh Lord, I can't—don't ask me—take somebody else.' Den

I could hear de Lord answer, 'It's you I want,

Harriet Tubman'—jess as clear I heard him

speak—an' den I'd go agen down South an'

bring up my brudders and sisters.'"

The majority of Mt. Everest climbers die *on the way down* from the summit. The road down is harder than the road up. In earlier chapters, when we talked about mentors, I said, "You cannot go on a Hero's Journey alone." That advice is true and should have prompted you to acquire mentors for your Journey. Not being alone on the Journey is also true at the very end of your Journey. Are you willing to share what you have learned? Are you willing to guide others?

After Paula R.'s daughter was well enough to return to high school, Paula could have sighed, hugged her family and stopped there. It would have been a good thing to do, and a welcome respite from the work it took to nurse her daughter back to health. But after attending a National Eating Disorders Association (NEDA) conference, Paula resolved to shine a light on eating disorders as a mental health issue that is still not fully understood. She has taken on the job of coordinating an annual NEDA walk in her home town. She uses that platform to communicate with other parents. "Often, parents feel a sense of isolation, guilt, and shame, compounding their sense of helplessness and despair. We come together to console, commiserate, and support. We understand and we care. It is not enough, but it is something."

Gwen C. found a unique combination of tutoring and encouragement that worked well for her to help her most difficult students enhance their learning and study skills:

I could really see a difference in the students'

view of what they thought they could achieve

102

once I changed my approach. I was sitting at my desk one evening, after all the kids had gone, feeling all proud and, honestly, a little smug, too, at how much improvement I was seeing in these kids. I thought that every kid should have this chance. Then I realized, Oh, selfish me. Every teacher needs these tools. Then every kid really will have a chance. I was determined to spread my ideas then.

You have worked *hard*. You built strength and resilience by enduring the Tests and Trials. You built a team and a community with your Mentors and Allies. You and your Journey widened to include a lot of other people. You learned that your accomplishment could be even greater as you shared it. You might be afraid. You might feel "I'm not good enough." That's my favorite. But withholding your message is like letting someone starve because you don't think you're a good enough cook.

Exercise—The Messenger of Stuff I Learned the Hard Way

I believe you have gotten to this point on your Hero's Journey because you are a messenger. Holocaust survivor and author Elie Wiesel saw his duty was to be a "messenger of the dead among the living," so the dead, and what happened to them, would never be forgotten. Wiesel's message, born out of a great human tragedy, is huge. But you have gone through Tests and Trials, too.

Don't minimize your pain; don't compare who suffered more. You know things. You have learned things the hard way, and you want to save others from the pain you experienced on your Journey. You can save at least one person some pain with your message, so it will be worth it. Here are some Lessons Learned from others who learned it the hard way, too:

- "Choose discomfort over resentment."—Dr. Brene Brown

- "What you think of me is none of my business."—Devon Crane

- "God, grant me the serenity to accept the things I cannot change . . ."—Reinhold Niebuhr

- "A burned bridge never got anyone from point A to point B."—Megan Shepherd

- "Never take a job just for a pay increase. You'll end up hating it. Life goes by so fast you can't even imagine it, so never stay in a job you hate."—Me.

Now, my Lesson Learned quote is not as short and pithy as the others, but my sentiment is true and heartfelt. Many years ago, I took a job as a database administrator, mostly because I could double my salary immediately, and parts of the job looked like they would be interesting to learn. After the training, where I did not do well by the way, I worked for a consulting company doing installations of the database at various companies. I never could quite get the hang of the work. I was frustrated nearly every day and didn't know what to do. The larger income did nothing to assuage my discouragement. Many mornings I would lie in bed, nearly in tears for what lay ahead that day. I would think, "I'll just call in and quit. I'll find something to do." Then I would drag myself to work, hating nearly every minute.

I had no earth-shaking moment that finally ended it, just dinner with a friend who responded to my woes with a temporary job offer, allowing me to change direction and learn that lesson. It was a painful year.

What have you learned the hard way that you want very much to share with others? It will take only a minute to write it down. Grab a pen and do it now!

Don't worry how long your Journey takes, or if you take more **Rest Stops** than "everybody else." You have seen by now that the Hero's Journey is not linear, and the stages are not uniform length or depth. You know by now that any Hero's Journey, including your own, is not one single task. The Journey requires you be acutely aware of your intent and goal, and those of the people around you. You start out with your goal based on *your* needs and *your* desires, following *your* bliss, but the Journey morphs and changes you in the process. Somewhere along the way you and your Journey evolved into something larger.

The marker of the Road Back stage is integrating your new knowledge and new self into the regular world. The regular world looks a little like the world you left, but it is forever changed by how *you* have changed.

Now that you are moving back into the regular world, you know you see things differently, but have you noticed that other people see *you* differently now? You have new allies and mentors who have become a part of your life. Some people who were your friends at the start of your Journey don't fit into your new life now. If you are on a Hero's Journey to resolve an addiction, you know you cannot maintain old "party" friendships, or you risk your own abstinence.

You probably had plenty of friends and family who thought this quest of yours was a bad idea. They might still think that. They may even express their opinion loudly that you are just a little too big for your britches now. Being judged and ostracized by people you love is the main reason many people don't finish their Hero's Journey. I can't blame them for giving up when faced with losing approval and what had always seemed like love. But . . . if you can find a way to accept those losses and keep moving toward your goal, we will continue on.

What do you need to do today to keep moving on your Hero's Journey?

Since you decided to trudge the Road Back and keep going, you have to refine and clearly state your message for others. Remember what you have learned on this Journey. Remember how you have grown and changed. Your very smallest minimum message is "I did it, and you can, too."

Chapter 12. A New Version of You is Resurrected

*"I stopped pretending to myself that I was
anything other than what I was and began to
direct all my energy into finishing the only work
that mattered to me."*—J. K. Rowling

What's This Hero's Journey Stage About?

In this stage, your new "you" emerges. This version of you has been tempered by your Tests and Trials and is Resurrected with new skills, new wisdom, and greater vision to bring back to your village.

One result of your Tests and Trials is that you have had to give up your attachment to your limitations and fears. You've been pushed beyond what the old you thought you could do. Those limited parts of you die off a little more with each step you take to fulfill your goal.

You become connected to truth and "all that is" in those moments when you no longer resist the inevitable death required to resurrect yourself as the Hero of your own Journey. When you make it this far, you are reborn as a *better* you. Discovering this truth about yourself is the purpose of your Hero's Journey.

Perhaps that's why some people get stuck on the Road Back. They intuitively know that as they get to the end of the Journey, they will no longer be the Hero, and they must change and take on a new role. Allowing the destruction of your "self" as the Hero so you can morph into a new identity takes even more courage than that first step out onto your Hero's Journey did. Now you know what's out there and how challenging it is.

You may emerge as a mystic, sage, teacher, healer, mentor, or advocate. Your new identity may be wide-ranging, and include several of those roles. Long-buried aspects of your self have come out while you were on the Journey. You are like the storied phoenix, the magical bird that rises from its own ashes. Jana has been conducting workshops for women while she finishes her book. She says:

> I really feel like I'm growing into my new and larger self. I've faced long term problems that stopped me from doing things I want to do in my life. I've become stronger and much more "me" than before. Although I'm not yet behind that final curtain—I still have to bring my message home, but I'm close to it—I can see how I'm more courageous, a much more whole and integrated person. It's so beneficial to support each other on this Journey, isn't it?

Sylvia told me:

> I thought my Journey was about beating the government and the insurance companies. I loved it every time I helped someone get their claim approved or we got a special hearing or an exception [to a denied claim]. I would pump my fist and whoop! But one day a client just looked at me and said, "They're just doing the best they can. They're people, too." I'd been so used to fighting, fighting, fighting my own cancer I

didn't know how to stop fighting. I was fighting everybody. I didn't even get it, though, that day. It took me a couple more weeks to shift. I'm stubborn.

Janet says she is inspired to support people.

When someone mentions they are struggling, I immediately encourage them now. I cheer them on, because the mentors, teachers and cheerleaders were so important to me. And not the fake-y "Oh, that's nice, good luck with that" response, but I really look into the eyes and heart of that person and say, "Yes, you are a big deal and you can do this." We don't know when something we say will be a deciding factor or really help someone.

Paula says she's always been a judgmental person.

One of my favorite quotes was (and still is): "You can visit pity city but you can't live there." My Journey through my daughter's mental illness and advocacy for others with the NEDA walk has given me a completely different perspective. Mental illnesses can be debilitating and life-threatening, and it is not always possible to "snap out of it" through sheer will power. I can see I'm more empathetic and less judgmental of others from this.

Gwen has created a summer class in the Washington, D.C., area, for elementary school teachers like herself who want to be the most powerfully, encouraging mentors they can be. "My new goal is accreditation for my class. Once I have that, I can really make a huge impact, but I am happy with every person I reach."

Carl Jung said, "I made it the task of tasks of my own life to find by what mythology I was living." He states an excellent goal. By what mythology are *you* living? I interpret this statement as: What is the story you tell of your life? Let me amend that: What is the story you tell yourself of your life? What are you doing now to create a myth by which you want to live?

Have you answered your Call to Adventure?

Have you followed your bliss?

Let's both undertake the final stages of our Journey.

LA BELLE ET LA BÊTE—BEAUTY AND THE BEAST

In the traditional French story, Beauty and the Beast, two characters undertake a Hero's Journey.

As the result of his spoiled and selfish behavior, a magical spell transformed a prince into a hideous beast. Along his Hero's Journey, the Beast meets Belle (Beauty), who demonstrates kindness and generosity despite his cold treatment. She causes him to imagine the Hero he could become.

Belle has her own Hero's Journey when she volunteers to go to the Beast's castle to live alone with him and fulfill the bargain the Beast made to spare her father's life. Belle shows unconditional love, kindness, and willingness to look beyond the Beast's physical appearance. In a test of her fidelity, the Beast sends her home to visit her family one last time. While away from him, she dreams he is dying and realizes she has come to love him. She willingly leaves her family to return to what she believes is an isolated life with the Beast. Her selfless act of love lifts the enchantment. The Beast is redeemed and sheds the skin of his former self to be transformed, not only back into human form but into an unselfish and loving prince.

The crucial act that triggers your Resurrection on your Hero's Journey is atonement. In this stage of the Journey, in classical stories, the Hero reaches atonement with his father or father-figure. All throughout your Journey you have been reconnecting long-abandoned or lost parts of your self. You are ready for atonement with whatever or whoever holds the ultimate power in your life. (Spoiler alert: it's you.)

First, we need to look at the words *atone* and *atonement*. Don't slip into the colloquial meaning that has you punishing yourself for anything. Even if you have done things in the past that need fixing, hurting and punishing yourself won't help. The word *atone* means "reparation for a wrong or injury." Repairing. *Re-pairing*. The action of putting back together; integrating something that has been pulled apart. Atonement, therefore, is as the *Oxford English Dictionary* says, "To reconcile hymselfe and make an onement with god [sic]."

Because I believe we are always one with all that is (we just forget frequently), the act of atonement is remembering and acknowledging our one-ness again. Atonement is integrating all of our parts and seeing the whole we've really always been all along. For your on-purpose Hero's Journey, you know you must do all you can to reconcile and repair those "parts" you've abandoned.

What have you overcome on this Journey that had great power in your life? Was it expectations you felt everyone laid onto you, or expectations you laid onto yourself? Did you give great power to your limitations or self-ascribed shortcomings?

I was a part of a group guided meditation a few months ago and, near the end, the facilitator said, "Tell that orphaned part of you, I want you with me always."

That phrase pulled me out of the blissful place I had been and repulsed me. I wondered why I had such a strong reaction, so I wrote the phrase down. I re-read it nearly every day for months before I garnered the gumption to explore it.

One evening I decided to see where my reaction came from, so I did a visioning meditation. In it, I saw the orphaned me as weak and frightened, and I was ashamed of her. When I pictured a little orphaned me standing beside me on a sidewalk, I was disgusted. I was repelled by her weakness and vulnerability when she had been hurt, lonely, and felt abandoned. I felt my anger pulse out to everyone around me, because I was ashamed of this weak part of myself. I pushed my anger out in a giant shock wave of emotion, like a nuclear blast that shook the buildings around us.

And then I realized, Oh! I have it backwards! I've been doing it backwards my whole life. So, I shifted the feeling and inverted the wave of emotion to circle back to a surge of love for the orphaned me. I felt a sonic blast of compassion for us both.

I had never recognized that the source of a lot of my anger was a shield, so that no one would see the scared and weak part of me. I can now acknowledge the orphaned me, hold her hand, and, yes, I can keep her beside me always. I feel only love for her.

I wish I could say this one visioning cured me of all of my anger. I really wish that were true! But at least now I catch myself more quickly when I'm angry and notice that I'm trying to hide my fear. Every day I take another little step toward atonement.

Exercise—Loving the Disowned Part

This exercise reads simply, but I'll be honest--it can be hard to do. You must be ready to do it. You must want the result of at-one-ment. You may want to do this exercise several times to work up to the final part.

Find a quiet place and time.

Ask yourself, "What part of me am I hiding from everyone? What do I not want anyone to see in me? If my friends and family knew, what would happen to me?"

Imagine opening a door and seeing the hidden part of you there. What do you feel when you see her?

When you can, take her by the hand and bring her out to stand in the sunshine. If you can't take her by the hand, ask her to come out on her own or motion her out.

Imagine your closest ally on your Hero's Journey there with you both. Introduce your friend to her. Admit you have been hiding her from your friend. For example, you may say, "Susanne, this is my orphan who is very weak and scared others will hurt her. I've never let you see her before, but I want you two to meet because I trust you will be kind to her."

If you can't introduce her, let your friend share your space with no words.

When you can, imagine that another ally or your mentor on your Hero's Journey comes into the room now to be with you all. Introduce your mentor to her. Admit you have been hiding her from your ally/mentor.

You can repeat the process a few more times, but bring in only fully trusted allies and your mentor. You don't need to share this part of you with friends or family.

The goal of this exercise is to bring disparate parts of *you* together and integrate parts you have been ignoring or pushing aside. When you are able to get through the step where you admit you have been hiding this part of yourself from a trusted friend, you will have repaired those separated parts of yourself and made at-one-ment. Now this really is the new you Resurrected from the Trials of your Journey.

What do you need to do today to keep moving on your Hero's Journey?

Remember you don't have to *do* anything to be one with everything. Take a moment now and let down all of the barriers you put up to block this awareness. Feel the connection and hold on to it, if only for a moment.

Chapter 13. Sharing Your Magic with the Village

"To be human is to become visible while carrying what is hidden as a gift to others . . ."—David Whyte, *from the poem* "What to Remember When Waking"

Are you ready to share what you have learned on your Hero's Journey?

Are you willing, knowing what you know now about how hard the Journey was, to bring others along?

Are you able to keep one foot in each world once you have completed a Journey?

PETER AND WENDY

In the Peter Pan story, the eponymous Peter is not the Hero of the story. Wendy Darling is the Hero. Wendy and her brothers follow Peter out of the nursery and over to Neverland for some amazing and terrifying adventures: Pirates! Fairies! Indians! But Peter stays in Neverland and remains a boy forever, while Wendy and her brothers decide to return home.

At the end of the story, Peter shows up at the nursery window again, but this time it is an adult Wendy who greets him. Time has stood still for

him, but not for her. She is now the mother to
the sleeping child in the nursey. She has
brought her experience and the stories of her
youthful courage to share with her children.

Once you decided to travel the Road Back, you knew
you were returning to the real world. Even if you lollygagged on
the Road Back, your world is different now.

You knew you would have to leave behind the fantastic
and return to the Ordinary World. Sometimes that's a painful
decision. But you decided to come back because you have magic
and a message to share with others. Others may already be
seeking you out.

Campbell said that *story* is key to personal fulfillment.
We must be able to tell our story; telling our story validates that
we are part of a "meaningful narrative," that our own personal
Journey is woven into the larger fabric of human experience.
Sometimes your story is the great gift you must share with the
village, and your reason to return.

In Mills's *The Adventure Gap*, he recounts the story of a
2013 expedition of the first all African-American team climb of
the Alaskan mountain, Denali. Over the weeks of climbing,
camp set-up, and dealing with mercurial weather, the nine
bonded, as a team of climbers must do to reach the summit
intact.

On the morning the team left camp at 19,000 feet to
climb their final segment to the summit, and with the summit in
view, an intense high-electrical thunderstorm rolled over Denali.
With a blizzard of snow, lightning crashing nearly next to them,
and their metal equipment and bodies buzzing with the
electricity in the air around them, they turned away from the
summit and started back down the mountain.

The main goal of the team's climb had been to bring the attention of people of color models of mountain climbers and adventurers. In fact, all the team members had committed to telling their experiences and encouraging others of color to "aspire to a life of adventure" when they returned home. Although they all regretted not being able to summit Denali (that time) they reveled in the joy of their entire team getting back to camp safely. "They would all live to climb another day" because they had put the group's safety before their own egos. That's an equally powerful message.

Now that you have made the full cycle of your Hero's Journey, you have lived in both the Ordinary World and the fantastic world. You have earned the ability to move back and forth between the two worlds, and you have learned this lesson through your Trials and your Ordeal.

Completing your Hero's Journey is you writing your own grand story—an epic just like *The Odyssey*. Your story is filled with great meaning for you and all who were a part of your Journey.

Unfortunately, most stories don't tell us what happened after the Hero returns home or after the fairy tale ends. In stories, the character doesn't get to decide what happens next. You do. What do you want to be your "happily ever after?"

Option 1: Take on the Mentor role. In the same way that you may have many different mentors, you will make a great mentor to others. Your mentor role may arise seamlessly as you reach the end of your Journey.

From the mentor role, you will learn invaluable lessons for your own future Journeys. You have the skills to be a powerful mentor and ally for someone on their Hero's Journey. You know what the stages feel like. You have learned that, although you can't skip a stage, you can pull yourself out when you get stuck in a stage. You know more than most people how

117

critical helpers are. It's time to give that gift to someone, as you have let others give the gift of helping to you.

Option 2: Document your Journey. Many famous Hero's Journeys are documented in the stories I've used in this book. Write your own story in whatever style you choose: an epic poem like Homer did for the *Iliad* and the *Odyssey* or a few lines of free verse. You can write a few paragraphs or an entire book, perhaps compose a song!

Have you been writing journal entries as you have traveled this Journey? If you look back you will likely clearly see your path and the lessons you have learned. If you haven't journaled along the way, you should take some time now and write the story of your Journey. Imagine being able to give your Hero's Journey story as a legacy to your family and friends.

Option 3: Prepare for a new Journey. As I said at the very beginning, you have already done this. Now you've completed at least two Journeys. You should take your time to decide what your next adventure will be. What's next for you? Start a spin-off from your current Journey? Or create something brand new?

A Hero's Journey is fractal, meaning there're many, many Journeys layered onto your life. The pattern repeats on those layers. Some Journeys are bigger and more physically trying than others. Some seem small only when you're inside the Journey, but when you complete it, you notice how wide it was—how many people were affected and how much it changed your life.

Option 3: Both! Whether at the same time, or alternating, you are now fully equipped to become a mentor *and* start a new Journey.

I hope you'll take some time for a **Rest Stop** and reflect on what you have accomplished and what you would enjoy doing next. Now that you are certain you can do it, you could even decide to push yourself to an even bigger risk and a greater reward.

You can see now, too, that the Journey is circular, but also spiral—you don't stay on the same level. Even if you haven't fully completed the Journey, you will likely start another one, and this new one layers into a Journey that is at a higher level *for you*. The new Journey will be more expanded, more evolved, it will call upon you in greater and deeper ways--but that new Journey starts where you are, at the point of your return to the village.

Looking back now that you have completed this Hero's Journey, can you see more clearly how we do the Hero's Journey throughout our lives? I believe our human experience is perfectly aligned to the Hero's Journey. We are meant to experience all of these stages in the course of simply living, and they give our lives more depth and greater meaning. Higher highs and lower lows, yeah . . . but worth it.

As I write this and look out the window, I see a hawk circling several hundred feet above me in the gray, cloud-filled sky. Her steady circles remind me that I must persist as well, regardless of my emotional weather. Joseph Campbell said that the monomyth of the Hero's Journey was in consciousness, that "myth was nature talking." He was right about that. Perhaps it was just waiting for us. Perhaps it created us.

"I don't know where I'm going from here, but I promise

it won't be boring."—David Bowie

Acknowledgements

Thank you to everyone who helped me along my book writing Hero's Journey.

A special deep and resonating thank you to all of you who shared their Journey stories with me to use in this book.

Thank you to my writing groups, Tuesdays with Story in Madison, Wisconsin, and Barbara Sher's Write-Speak Program, especially Patty Newbold, for all of your feedback, support, and encouragement.

Thank you to a wonderful editor, Ed levy.

Thank you to all of my mentors and allies along the Journey. You all are my proof that you cannot complete a Hero's Journey alone.

Made in the USA
Middletown, DE
23 July 2018